# Contents

# 100 HISTORY LESSONS 7-11

*100 History Lessons: 7-11* provides a series of lessons which build upon the QCA Schemes of Work for History at Key Stage 2. Each chapter focuses on a key study unit from the Scheme of Work, including the newer adapted study units. The eight chapters are:
1. Invaders and settlers
2. Tudor times
3. The Second World War
4. Ancient Egypt
5. Victorian Britain
6. Ancient Greeks
7. The Aztecs
8. Indus Valley.

## History skills and concepts

A key focus of the lessons provided in this book is the development of historical skills and concepts through appropriate and enjoyable activities. The key skills and concepts that are required in the *National Curriculum for History in England and Wales* and which also apply to the Scottish curriculum for history are clearly identified for each lesson.

In order to aid planning, these essential historical skills and concepts are set out at the beginning of each chapter in a grid. These grids show at a glance how the topics, skills and concepts are mapped out through the book and give links to key historical objectives for each lesson

### EXAMPLE taken from 'Ancient Greeks'

|  | OBJECTIVES | MAIN ACTIVITY |
|---|---|---|
| **Lesson 5** | To know about characteristic features of the period studied. | Using role play and debate, children learn how democracy worked in Ancient Greece. |
| **Lesson 6** | To find out about the past from a variety of sources. | Children learn about the roles of men, women and children in Ancient Greece. |

## Lesson plans

In addition to listing key objectives for every activity, each lesson plan also outlines how to approach the activity, the resources that it requires, any information to aid preparation for teaching the lesson and guidance on assessment and how this relates to further planning. Concise background information which you may need to support your teaching of the lesson is also provided. Activities are sequenced and can be used as a whole unit of work, or they can be selected and used within your own existing scheme of work. Many of the lesson activities are accompanied by photocopiable sheets; these are clearly identified in the grids with the symbol 🅿.

## Differentiation

Each lesson plan includes suggested ways of differentiating activities for lower abilities and the more able children in a year group. Plans also discuss how lessons can be adapted for use with a different age group or for a wide age range within a mixed-age class.

# INTRODUCTION

Consideration is also given to children from different social and cultural backgrounds.

**History and the wider curriculum**
The lessons in this book are particularly focused towards fostering and developing creativity, especially through links made across the curriculum. History is an excellent vehicle through which to enrich the wider curriculum and in particular through its natural links with literacy, geography, ICT and citizenship. It provides children w

- refine their communication and information-processing skills in a range of contexts
- develop and extend their investigative and problem-solving skills, including using number and ICT, inside and outside the classroom
- participate in a range of independent and collaborative learning experiences, which extend their personal, social and study skills
- gain experiences that help them to make connections between themselves, their communities and the wider world
- develop awareness and understanding of a range of peoples and cultures and a respect for many different attitudes, views and beliefs
- recognise the need for a just and equitable society and their own role in making this possible
- explore current issues within an historical context to make sense of the world around them and develop the skills and attitudes necessary for active involvement as citizens.
(QCA, Innovating with History, www.qca.org.uk/history/innovating/wider_curriculum.htm)

A key feature of this book therefore are the links it makes with other curriculum areas, in particular literacy, geography and ICT. In keeping with the Primary Strategy, the chapters in this book that particularly make the connection with other areas of the curriculum are those that build upon the new QCA Schemes of Work. These units make use of cross-curricular links in adapting existing units or combining them with units of work from other subject areas. They are, at Key Stage 2, the units on Romans, Aztecs and Victorian Local History (see the QCA Innovating with History website found on www.qca.org.uk/history).

Geography features prominently, since at Key Stage 2 there is an emphasis on making use of the children's own locality and school, more distant localities, and on introducing the notion of maps, plans and globes. Art and design are areas widely used throughout the lessons, as a means of encouraging a creative response to learning and sometimes as an assessment opportunity. Drama is a part of the National Curriculum for English, which can enhance a history lesson and bring it to life. Through simulation and role play children have the opportunity to obtain first-hand experience of the feelings and emotions of people in past situations. Developing Speaking and Listening skills is a central feature of many of the lesson plans.

# CHAPTER 1

# Invaders and settlers

This chapter covers an extremely long span of history, almost 1000 years. It is a very complex time with major culture clashes. For this reason, the chapter begins by giving children an initial overview of the whole period, so that they can begin to see the long sweep of time. A number of groups are studied within this time period – the Celts, Romans, Anglo-Saxons and Vikings.

Once this overview has been provided, it is suggested that just one of the invaders is studied in more detail. The lessons in this chapter reflect this approach. Therefore, introductory activities that focus on the use of sources as part of an investigative approach are provided for each invader. These are accompanied by activities that look in more detail at one aspect of that group, or at a particularly significant event for that group.

| | OBJECTIVES | MAIN ACTIVITY |
|---|---|---|
| **Lesson 1** 🅿 | To identify and describe reasons for, and results of, historical events, situations and changes. | Children consider the reasons for invaders coming to Britain and take part in role-play activities. |
| **Lesson 2** 🅿 | To place events, people and changes into correct periods of time. | Children place dates, pictures and information on a class timeline. |
| **Lesson 3** | To find out about the past from an appropriate range of sources, including ICT-based sources. To communicate their knowledge in a variety of ways. | In groups, children use sources to find out about the Celts and draw a mind map of their findings. |
| **Lesson 4** 🅿 | To find out about the past from story and visual sources. To communicate their knowledge in a variety of ways. | Children learn about Boudicca and then create a sequence of pictures and text to retell what they have learned. |
| **Lesson 5** | To find out about the past from an appropriate range of sources, including ICT-based sources. To communicate their knowledge of history in a variety of ways. | In groups, children investigate the Romans using a variety of sources and draw a mind map or summary chart of their findings. |
| **Lesson 6** 🅿 | To recall, select and organise historical information. To communicate their knowledge in a variety of ways. | Children compare the Roman and Celtic ways of life and take part in role play. |
| **Lesson 7** | To find out about the past from an appropriate range of sources, including ICT-based sources. To communicate their knowledge in a variety of ways. | In groups, children use a variety of sources to find out about the Saxons, especially about riddles. |
| **Lesson 8** | To find out about the past from historic sites. To communicate their knowledge in a variety of ways. | Children research Sutton Hoo using the internet. They write museum notices for pictures of artefacts. |
| **Lesson 9** 🅿 | To find out about the past from story. | Children read a story about the Viking raid on Lindisfarne and draw pictures with captions showing what they have learned. |
| **Lesson 10** | To find out about the past from an appropriate range of sources, including ICT-based sources. To recall, select and organise historical information. | In groups, children research the Viking way of life using a variety of sources. |
| **Lesson 11** 🅿 | To find out about the past from story and written sources. To communicate their knowledge in a variety of ways. | Children learn about King Alfred from two sources and create newspaper-style reports. |
| **Lesson 12** | To find out about the past from an appropriate range of sources. To communicate their knowledge in a variety of ways. | Children learn about place names and the influence of the Vikings on language. |

# Patterns of invasion and settlement

## Objectives
● To identify and describe reasons for, and results of, historical events, situations and changes.

## Vocabulary
Romans, Saxons, Vikings

## Resources
Large globe; map of northern Europe, showing Roman, Anglo-Saxon and Viking routes to Britain; the photocopiable sheet 'Map of invaders and settlers' on page 19, one per child; OHP (optional).

## Links
NC English KS2: En1 (1) to speak with confidence; (2) to listen, understand and respond appropriately; (3) to talk effectively as members of a group; (4) to participate in a range of drama activities.
NC Geography KS2: (1a) to ask geographical questions; (2a) to use appropriate geographical vocabulary; (2c) to use maps.
NC PSHE & citizenship KS2: (2i) to appreciate the range of national, regional, religious and ethnic identities in the UK.

## Background
Native Britons, the Celts and other tribes who lived in Britain prior to the Roman invasion were subjected to constant attack and change on a grand scale. Just as the Celts tried to resist the Roman occupation, the Saxons, led by kings such as Alfred, tried to resist successive waves of Viking attacks, eventually agreeing to divide the country into two - the north being mostly under Viking rule, while the southern parts remained predominantly Saxon.

## Introduction
● Ensure the class has prior experience of reading different maps.
● Look at the photocopiable sheet 'Map of invaders and settlers' on page 19. Consider with the children why the invaders wanted to settle in Britain, where they came from and the different times in history that they invaded.

## Main teaching activity
● Ask the children why they think people kept invading Britain for such a long period of time.
● Talk about the reasons why the Romans invaded, for example, to expand their empire and to make proper towns. Explain how these might have been different from the Saxons' and Vikings' reasons.
● Make a list of reasons for each group of invaders on an OHP or whiteboard for the children to use for reference.
● Divide the class into six groups: three groups represent the Ancient Britons or Celts, one the Romans, one the Saxons and one the Vikings.
● Suggest the groups of Ancient Britons discuss the kinds of work that they would have done and then practise miming these jobs. Ideas might include digging, mowing or cutting trees.
● Ask each invading group to discuss amongst themselves what they would say to the Britons about their invasion, for example, the Romans might say that they are coming to improve the country and make a better way of life.
● Encourage each group of invaders to work together to prepare a short speech to make to one of the groups of Ancient Britons. Ask the Britons to respond, saying how they feel about being invaded.

## Plenary
● Role play the meetings between each group of Ancient Britons and the groups of invaders in chronological order.

## Differentiation
Provide additional adult support for children needing help with recalling the reasons and planning their actions and speeches.

# Invasion timeline

## Objectives
● To place events, people and changes into correct periods of time.

## Vocabulary
invaders, invasion, conquest

## Resources
Art materials; selection of illustrated reference books, the photocopiable sheet 'Map of invaders and settlers' on page 19; large blank timeline covering the period of the invasions, from 55BC to AD1066; the photocopiable sheet 'Event cards' on page 20, cut up and one set per group; set of blank cards cut to fit easily on the timeline.

## Links
NLS Y3 Word level work: vocabulary extension by collecting new words from reading and work in other subjects; to develop time-related language.
NLS Y3 T1 Text 17: to understand the distinction between fact and fiction; Y3 T1 Text 22: to make a simple record of information by completing a chart.
NNS Y3-4: number sequences, place value and ordering.
NC English KS2: En1 (1) to speak with confidence; (2) to listen, understand and respond appropriately; (3) to talk effectively as members of a group.

## Background
Children find time and chronology one of the most difficult concepts to grasp. This lesson uses a simple timeline in order to show children how and why events can be put into a sequence. It provides an opportunity to talk about the process of sequencing and encourages children to develop time-related language and an understanding of how dates are sequenced in the same way as a number line.

## Introduction
● Ask the class: *When did each group of invaders arrive? Which group came first?*
● Explain that the children are going to make a timeline to show the order in which the different groups of people invaded Britain.

## Main teaching activity
● Put the children into groups and assign each a group of invaders to investigate.
● Provide a set of 'Event cards' from the photocopiable sheet on page 20, blank cards, art materials and reference books for each group.
● Ask the children to make illustrations on their blank cards of their group of invaders, using the reference books for research.
● Revise the map on the photocopiable sheet on page 19. Look at the different times that the invaders arrived in Britain.
● Using the empty timeline, count along in steps of 100 and then in steps of ten years. Give the children practice in placing numbers in order, reading out the numbers and saying them as dates.
● Ask volunteers to place their event cards in the correct places on the timeline.
● Invite each child to place their own picture on the timeline.
● Add more information on cards, such as the different reasons for invasions that the children have learned, and ask the children to place these on the timeline, explaining why they have put them in particular places.
● Refer to the difference between fact and fiction, and ask which of these words describes the events on the timeline.

## Plenary
● Ask for individuals to give, in their own words, brief explanations of what the class timeline shows. Make sure that all the children have a good understanding of the long period of history that is covered on the timeline.

## Differentiation
Provide adult support for children who find it difficult to locate appropriate illustrations to draw. Ask the more able to make their own labels to accompany their pictures on the timeline.

# The Celtic way of life

## Background
The Celts, otherwise known in British history as the Ancient Britons, were the dominant peoples in pre-Roman times and their culture was widespread in Europe. There is a long history of their clashes with Rome and its advancing army, which eventually succeeded in pushing them into the more remote extremities of Europe on the fringes of the Roman Empire. The Celts are famous for their art, warfare, and distinctive clothes and houses.

## Introduction
● Tell the children that they are going to find out about people called the Celts and look especially at their art.
● Ask the children if they have heard of the word 'Celt' and discuss briefly when and where they lived.
● Encourage the children to begin to think of things that they would like to know about the Celts. Formulate a series of questions together, such as, *What was the Celtic way of life like?* and, *What can we find out from sources?* Write the questions on a whiteboard.

## Main teaching activity
● Allow time for the children to look at a range of sources about the Celts, such as pictures of people, a map showing the Celtic areas, photographs of artefacts and reconstructions of Celtic dwellings.
● Organise the class to work in groups. Refer to the list of questions on the whiteboard and give the children time to research answers to the questions and to discuss their findings in their groups.
● Ask the children to look for examples of Celtic art. Point out their use of pattern and design.
● Revise mind maps with the class and set the groups the task of drawing a mind map to show their findings.

## Plenary
● Ask each group to summarise what they have found out for the rest of the class. Complete a mind map on the whiteboard, to show how their findings can be classified under different aspects of Celtic life.
● Conclude by discussing the Celts now. What areas are still known as Celtic? Talk about names that still exist, such as Celtic Rangers, the football team.

## Differentiation
Adult support will be needed for the less able children when completing their mind map. Alternatively, provide a partially completed mind map for them to work on. For the children who work more quickly, provide artwork as an extension task. The children could create their own pictures and models using examples of Celtic art as a stimulus.

# Boudicca's rebellion

## Objectives
● How to find out about the events, people and changes studied from story and visual sources.
● To ask and answer questions, and to select and record information relevant to the focus of the enquiry.
● To recall, select and organise historical information.
● To communicate their knowledge and understanding of history in a variety of ways.

## Vocabulary
resistance, warrior queen

## Resources
The photocopiable sheet 'Queen Boudicca' on page 21; illustrations of Boudicca; strips of folded paper for each child (see diagram); art materials and pencils; OHP.

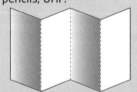

## Links
NLS Y3 Word level work: vocabulary extension by collecting new words from reading and work in other subjects.
NC English KS2: En1 (1) to speak with confidence; (2) to listen, understand and respond appropriately; (3) to talk effectively as members of a group.
NC Art and design KS2: (1a) to record from experience and imagination.

## Background
Boudicca was a Queen of the Iceni tribe, who, along with her daughters, had been very harshly treated at the hands of the Romans, following the death of her husband, King Prasutagus. She therefore had two good motives for trying to resist Roman rule, both personal and political ones. In Celtic cultures, women were considered equally able to rule and to lead and, therefore, Boudicca's tribe's people had no hesitation in responding to her calls to fight the invaders. They too felt there was a need to resist the Roman settlement of Britain.

## Introduction
● Look at the pictures of Boudicca with the class. Ask if any of the children have heard of Boudicca before. What do they already know about her? Why did she attack the Romans?
● Explain that you are going to try to find out as much as possible about Boudicca from a story about her.

## Main teaching activity
● Read the photocopiable sheet 'Queen Boudicca' on page 21 to the children. Discuss what happens in the story.
● Ask the class questions about Boudicca based on the passage they have just heard. Explain any unfamiliar words and place names.
● Ask the children for reasons for Boudicca's behaviour, for example, she desired revenge because she had suffered humiliation at the hands of the Romans.
● Display a copy of the story on an OHP so that the children can refer to it. Give the children strips of folded paper and art materials to make into a series of pictures showing Boudicca's story.
● Make sure that the children understand that they need to retell the story in the correct sequence of events. Help the children to choose suitable subjects to illustrate as necessary for the individuals in the class.
● Encourage the children to write relevant captions or sentences underneath their illustrations. If there is time, invite the children to draw 'covers' on the front page to create a book of Queen Boudicca.

## Plenary
● Help the children to make a 3D display of their story sequences, and read through some of them together.

## Differentiation
Less able learners will need more adult support in creating their picture sequences. They may need shorter sequences to work on, including only three or four events rather then the fuller version. More able writers will be able to add longer pieces of text to their sequences.

# The Roman way of life

## Objectives
● To find out about the events, people and changes studied from an appropriate range of sources of information, including ICT-based sources.
● To recall, select and organise historical information.
● To communicate their knowledge and understanding of history in a variety of ways.

## Vocabulary
artefacts, pictures, stories, accounts

## Resources
Variety of information books on the Romans, photopacks and resource packs containing illustrations and written sources; suitable websites, such as www.brims.co.uk/romans/

## Links
NLS Y3 T2 Text 17: to make clear notes.
NC English KS2: En1 (1) to speak with confidence; (2) to listen, understand and respond appropriately; (3) to talk effectively as members of a group.
NC ICT KS2: (1a) to talk about what information they need and how they can find and use it; (1b) select suitable resources and find information.
NC Art and design KS2: (1a) to record from experience and imagination.

## Background
Julius Caesar's famous visit to Britain in 55bc and the eventual invasion in AD43 were the beginnings of the establishment of Roman rule in Britain which lasted for approximately 400 years. The Romans brought, among other things, a different language, new styles of building, dress and way of life. Some of their major pieces of architecture are still visible today and many traces of their occupation can be found in place names and in modern English words.

## Introduction
● Tell the children they are going to find out about people called the Romans and especially about their buildings, statues and sculptures.
● Ask the children what they have already heard about the Romans and list answers on the board.
● Explain that they are now going to find out more for themselves, and invite suggestions as to what they would like to know.
● Prompt them with questions such as: *What was it like to live in Roman times? What would we like to find out about what they did?*

## Main teaching activity
● Provide a range of sources about the Romans for the children to look at, for example: pictures and photographs of Roman buildings and artefacts, illustrations of Roman people and soldiers, showing their dress, photographs or models of statues and sculptures.
● Organise the sources into categories, such as pictures of people and buildings, photographs of artefacts, and short written accounts. Place these on different tables.
● Divide the children into groups and give each group just one type of source. Ask them to summarise in brief notes what they can say about the Romans from their understanding of the sources on their table.
● After a specified time, ask the children to move to another table and swap their findings with that group.
● Work round the groups, until they have 'snowballed' all their information, so that the whole class has a summary of all the findings.

## Plenary
● Working with the whole class, make a summary chart or mind map of the children's findings, using suggestions from each group in turn. Discuss the value of each type of source used and which they thought was the best for finding out what they wanted to know.

## Differentiation
Group the class according to ability for the group work. Select suitable sources, for example, pictures for the less able and longer pieces of text for the better readers. Extension activities could include making sketches of Roman architecture or making sculptures from clay.

11

# A comparison of Celtic and Roman ways of life

## Objectives
● To recall, select and organise historical information.
● To communicate their knowledge and understanding of history in a variety of ways.

## Vocabulary
compare, similar, different

## Resources
Mind maps or summary charts from Lessons 3 and 5, if appropriate; the photocopiable sheet 'Celtic and Roman ways of life compared' on page 22, one per child; variety of reference books and resource packs.

## Links
NLS Y3 Word level work: vocabulary extension by collecting new words from reading and work in other subjects.
NLS Y3 T2 Text 17: to make clear notes.
NC English KS2: En1 (1) to speak with confidence; (2) to listen, understand and respond appropriately; (3) to talk effectively as members of a group; (4) to participate in a range of drama activities.

## Background
Ideally this and Lessons 3, 4 and 5 should be taught in sequence. Alternatively, information about the Celts and Romans, summarised into a suitable format, will need to be made available for the children to use during this lesson.

## Introduction
● Explain to the class that they are going to think about how the Celtic and Roman ways of life were similar and different.

## Main teaching activity
● If appropriate, talk with the class about their findings from Lessons 3 and 5. Give each child a copy of the photocopiable sheet 'Celtic and Roman ways of life compared' on page 22.
● Work with the whole class to discuss the things that were the same and different about the two groups of people. Search other sources of information to find further similarities and differences and ask the children to complete the sheet. Discuss their answers together.
● Organise the children into groups and set them the task of role playing Romans and Celts, half of the group as Romans and the other half as Celts.
● Give the 'Romans' Roman names, such as Julius, Cassius, Antonius, Octavius and Hadrian (for the boys) and Diana, Vesta, Annia, Cornelia and Antonia (for the girls); give the 'Celts' Celtic names, such as Branwen, Fiona, Gilda, Erin and Nola (girls) and Conan, Weland, Bodvoc, Marbod and Verica (boys).
● Allow some time for the children to look at and discuss the characteristic features of each group and then rehearse their role play together; for example, the 'Romans' could explain how they like to go to the baths every day.
● Ensure that each group decides on a relevant topic area to role play and that each child within the group takes part in the activity. Extra adult helpers will be useful to provide additional support.

## Plenary
● Ask each group in turn to present their role play to the other children. If possible, make a video of their work to use in the future. If there is time, ask the children to discuss what they have discovered from watching and taking part in the role plays.
● Encourage the children to consider which way of life they think would have been preferable.

## Differentiation
Use mixed-ability groups to support quieter children for the role play.

# The Saxon way of life

## Objectives
● To find out about events, people and changes studied from an appropriate range of sources of information, including ICT-based sources.
● To recall, select and organise historical information.
● To communicate their knowledge and understanding of history in a variety of ways.

## Vocabulary
Angles, Saxons, Jutes

## Resources
Variety of information books on the Anglo-Saxons, photopacks and resource packs containing illustrations and written sources, such as riddles (www.abdn.ac.uk/english/beowulf/riddle.htm has good examples); suitable websites such as www.bbc.co.uk/schools/anglosaxons/

## Links
NLS Y3 Word level work: vocabulary extension by collecting new words from reading.
NLS Y3 T2 Text 17: to make clear notes.
NC English KS2: En1 (1) to speak with confidence; (2) to listen, understand and respond appropriately; (3) to talk effectively as members of a group.
NC ICT KS2: (3a) to share information in a variety of forms; (4a) to review what they and others have done.

## Background
The Anglo-Saxons were made up of a number of different tribes, which included the Saxons, Angles and Jutes. The Saxon tribes began to attack the coasts of Britain following the withdrawal of the Roman armies around AD410. Each group eventually settled in a different part of the country, the Angles the north and east of England, the Jutes in Kent and Hampshire, and the Saxons, in the areas now known as Sussex, Essex, Middlesex, Hampshire and Devon (Devon was then known as 'Wessex'). Much of Scotland, Wales, Ireland and Cornwall remained under the control of Celtic tribes. Also, the Saxon tribes were constantly under threat from the waves of attack mounted by the Vikings. These raids were recorded in detail in a contemporary source compiled over many years, known as the Anglo-Saxon Chronicle.

## Introduction
● Invite the class to say what they have heard about the people called the Saxons. Make a note of what they know.
● Ask if they have heard of any famous people from Saxon times, for example, King Alfred, the Venerable Bede, St Augustine. Explain that they are going to find out from sources what the Saxon way of life was like, and especially look at their riddles. Explain that riddles were popular in Anglo-Saxon times.

## Main teaching activity
● Provide the children with a range of sources organised into categories, such as pictures of people, photographs of artefacts and historic sites, and short written accounts or riddles.
● Arrange the children into groups and give each group just one type of source and ask them to discuss what they can learn or guess about the Anglo-Saxons from their sources. For example, from the riddles they can work out that the Anglo-Saxons had a good sense of humour and that they liked to play games.
● Set the children the task of summarising in brief notes what they can say from their understanding of the sources on their table.

## Plenary
● Ask the children to share all of their findings. Write up notes of all their information, as shared writing on the whiteboard, so that the whole class has a summary.

## Differentiation
Select suitable sources for children of different abilities, for example, pictures for the less able and longer pieces of text for the better readers. As an extension activity set the children the task of finding some Anglo-Saxon riddles from the internet or creating their own riddles to try out on the class.

# Sutton Hoo

## Objectives
- To find out about the events, people and changes studied from historic sites.
- To recall, select and organise historical information.
- To communicate their knowledge and understanding of history in a variety of ways.

## Vocabulary
burial, mound, archaeologist

## Resources
Map of England; OHP (optional); large scale map of the area around Sutton Hoo and aerial photograph; pens and paper; variety of resources about Sutton Hoo, such as information books, photopacks and resource packs containing illustrations and written sources for the class to use; suitable websites, including www.thebritish museum.ac.uk/ childrenscompass/

## Links
NLS Y3 Word level work: vocabulary extension by collecting new words.
NLS Y3 T3 Text 20: to write notes linked to work in other subjects.
NC Geography KS2: (2c) to use maps and plans at a range of scales.
NC ICT KS2: (1a) to talk about what information they need and how they can find and use it; (1b) to select suitable resources and find information.

## Background
Sutton Hoo is famous for its Anglo-Saxon burial mounds. These burials are thought to have been robbed in the Middle Ages and then excavated for curiosities in the 19th century. During the 20th century there were three major archaeological excavations, which have uncovered vast treasures.

Mound One is the most famous of the burial chambers, containing a ship burial in which were found the remains of a warrior king, possibly King Redwald. The treasure hoards would have been buried, as was the custom, along with the king. The metalwork on some objects shows that they came from other parts of Europe, indicating that the Vikings had travelled far afield. Most of the treasures that were found can be seen on the British Museum website.

## Introduction
- Ask if the children have heard of Sutton Hoo. Do they know what is there?
- Show the children a map of England and help them locate Sutton Hoo. (It is near to Woodbridge, Suffolk.)
- Explain how there have been many attempts to discover what was buried there, and tell the children what was found during the last century by archaeologists.
- Say the children are going to consider what the objects found at Sutton Hoo tell us about the Anglo-Saxons.

## Main teaching activity
- Using an overhead projector or whiteboard, look at a large scale map and aerial photograph of the Sutton Hoo site, and discuss what can be seen, for example, the burial mounds.
- Point out Mound One and show pictures of what this looked like after it had been excavated. Look at artefacts with the class, using the website: www.thebritishmuseum.ac.uk/childrenscompass/.
- Provide the children with a range of photographs of the artefacts found at Sutton Hoo, dividing them one for each child or one per pair.
- Ask the children to write some text about their picture, in the style of a museum notice, explaining in a few sentences what it tells us about the Saxons.

## Plenary
- Ask the children to show their picture and read out the notice they have written about their artefact and what it says about the Saxons.

## Differentiation
Provide sentence starters and word cards to support the less able writers during the writing activity. Encourage more able children to write longer pieces about their artefact.

# Longboats at Lindisfarne

## Background
Viking longboats were skilfully made, built especially for attacking other lands. They were made of wood and designed in a very narrow, streamlined shape for speed. They often had a steeply curved prow surmounted by a striking figurehead. They could hold up to 200 warriors. In AD793, the first major Viking attack took place on the island of Lindisfarne in Northumberland. Longboats arrived and the attackers slaughtered the monks and priests they found in the monastery, which was the main building on the peaceful island. Showing no mercy, they burned, looted and killed in the surrounding area. Finding little resistance, they soon returned and gradually began to attack more widely.

Prior to the lesson, create from card a large picture of a longboat. Fix it to the display board so that it projects out in a curved shape.

## Introduction
● Explain to the class that people from Scandinavia often sailed far around the world. They are known to have travelled widely in Europe and Asia, and even to have landed on the coast of North America, long before it was 'discovered' by Columbus.
● Tell the children how the first Viking raid on England took place.
● Tell them that in this lesson they are going to look at the question: *What can we find out about Lindisfarne from story?*
● Explain that they are going to find out especially about the Vikings' longboats.

## Main teaching activity
● Look at a map of northern England and point out Lindisfarne.
● Give the children a copy of the photocopiable sheet 'The Viking raid on Lindisfarne' on page 23. Read the story in a shared reading session.
● Challenge the children to find, from the story, information about the Vikings, such as: what sort of people were in the invading force; what did they wear; what were their ships like; what did they look like; what did they do; what happened to the Saxons that were attacked?
● Research Viking longboats together, using a variety of sources and the 'Background information' above.
● Give out cards or paper cut to a suitable size for display, for the children to record their findings as pictures and captions around the longboat on the wall.

## Plenary
● Review the children's verbal and pictorial answers. Discuss with the class whether this story is based on fact or fiction, and how we know.

## Differentiation
Differentiate support and questions during the story-reading session.

# The Viking way of life

## Objectives
● To find out about the events, people and changes studied from an appropriate range of sources of information, including ICT-based sources.
● To recall, select and organise historical information.
● To communicate their knowledge and understanding of history in a variety of ways.

## Vocabulary
sources, evidence, Scandinavia

## Resources
Map of Northern Europe; a variety of information books, for example: *Exploring the Vikings* by John Malam (Evans Brothers), photopacks and resource packs containing illustrations and written sources for the class to use; suitable websites, such as www.bbc.co.uk/schools/vikings/

## Links
NLS Y3 T2 Text 17: to make clear notes.
NC English KS2: En1 (1) to speak with confidence; (2) to listen, understand and respond appropriately; (3) to talk effectively as members of a group.
NC ICT KS2: (1a) to talk about what information they need and how they can find and use it; (1b) to select suitable resources and find information.
NC Geography KS2: (2c) to use globes and maps

## Background
The Vikings originated from a number of different Scandinavian regions, including Sweden, Norway and Denmark. Their empire was large during the 11th century, covering much of the western European coastline. They are known to have settled in France, Spain and Ireland, as well as in England.

## Introduction
● Explain to the class the lesson objectives – they are going to find answers to the following questions: *What was the Viking way of life like? What can we find out from sources?*
● Talk about how, if time allows, they will find out about Viking warriors in particular.

## Main teaching activity
● Look at the map of Northern Europe to see where the Vikings came from and trace their sea routes to England.
● Give the children a range of sources about the Vikings to look at. Organise the sources into categories, such as pictures of people, photographs of artefacts and historic sites, and short written accounts.
● Organise the children into groups and give each group just one type of source and ask them appropriate questions, such as: *What sort of things did the Vikings make? What were their homes like?*
● Then ask the groups to summarise in brief notes what they can say from their understanding of the sources on their table.
● After a specified time, ask the children to share their findings and write up, as whole-class shared writing, notes of all their information so that all the children have a summary of their findings.
● Use the resources to learn more about Viking warriors, referring to the photocopiable sheet 'The Viking raid on Lindisfarne' on page 23 if appropriate and time allows. Encourage the children to consider not just the fighting, but the warrior way of life, including burial rites, Viking myths and sagas, and so on.

## Plenary
● Together consider the key features of Viking life and discuss how this differs or is the same as life today.

## Differentiation
Provide adult support for the less able writers during the shared writing time. Encourage more able children to complete longer pieces of writing and to choose a topic to cover in depth.

# King Alfred and the Danes

## Objectives
● To find out about the events, people and changes studied from story and written sources.
● To recall, select and organise historical information.
● To communicate their knowledge and understanding of history in a variety of ways.

## Vocabulary
chronicle, King Alfred, Danes, raids

## Resources
The photocopiable sheet 'Extract from the Anglo-Saxon Chronicle' on page 24, displayed on an OHP; the photocopiable sheet 'A story about King Alfred' on page 25, one per child; large sheets of paper; pens and drawing materials.

## Links
NC English KS2: En1 (1) to speak with confidence; (2) to listen, understand and respond appropriately; (3) to talk effectively as members of a group; (4) to participate in a range of drama activities.
NC Geography KS2: (2c) to use globes and maps.

## Background
King Alfred is renowned as the Saxon ruler who finally brought a conclusion to the Viking raids. Much can be found out about these raids and about Alfred's responses to them from the *Anglo-Saxon Chronicle*. However, this can be a difficult source for young children to understand so the photocopiable sheet on page 25 summarises some of the events and tells the story of Alfred and the burning loaves.

## Introduction
● Briefly talk to the children about the Viking raids and how the Vikings would sail up rivers like the Thames to attack major towns. Explain that the raids had gone on for hundreds of years until at last one Saxon king found a way of dealing with the problem.
● Tell the children that they are going to read two kinds of source about what happened.
● They are going to answer the questions: *What can we find out about King Alfred from story and from the Anglo-Saxon Chronicle?* and *What can we find out about King Alfred from stories?*

## Main teaching activity
● Read the photocopiable sheet 'Extract from the Anglo-Saxon Chronicle' on page 24 to the children.
● Encourage the children to empathise with the Saxons under attack – what would it have felt like? Discuss the problems that Alfred faced.
● Discuss how Guthrum the Dane, who was a pagan, agreed to be baptised a Christian and how Alfred was careful to come to terms with the Vikings in order to save his kingdom.
● Read together the story on the photocopiable sheet on page 25. Explain that this source is a modern retelling.
● Ask the children to think how the wife might have felt when she realised she had scolded the king.
● Invite one of the children (or an adult helper) to take the role of the wife and to be interviewed by the rest of the class, acting as 'reporters' for a newspaper.
● Give out sheets of paper and pens and ask the children to write and illustrate a 'newspaper report' of the incident of King Alfred and the burning loaves.

## Plenary
● Discuss whether the children think Alfred was right to make an agreement with the Vikings. Ask them what else he might have done.

## Differentiation
Create a framework for the newspaper report for less able children. More able children could extend the writing activity to include other events, for example, Guthrum's baptism.

# Viking place names

## Objectives
● To find out about the events, people and changes studied from an appropriate range of sources of information.
● To communicate their knowledge and understanding of history in a variety of ways.

## Vocabulary
-thwaite, -toft, -thorpe

## Resources
Copy of the groups of place names (in the background notes) for each child; map of Britain; computer access (optional).

## Background

For nearly 300 years the Vikings were a powerful influence on England. They particularly left their mark on the language, which still has words and place names that have come from the Vikings. Often, the endings of place names tell you that they are from Viking times:

| | |
|---|---|
| -by = farm or village<br>Coningsby - king's village<br>Denby - Danes' village<br>Ingleby - village of the English<br>Selby - willow farm | -thwaite = clearing, meadow or field<br>Applethwaite - apple tree clearing<br>Brackenthwaite - bracken clearing<br>Kirkthwaite - church field |
| -thorpe = hamlet or small village<br>Burythorpe - hill hamlet<br>Grassthorpe - grass hamlet<br>Scunthorpe - Skuma's hamlet | -toft = homestead<br>Bratoft - broad homestead<br>Lowestoft - Hlothver's homestead<br>Nortoft - north homestead |

## Introduction

● Look at the list of place names together. Ask the children to say their own surnames. Do any of these end in '-by', or '-thwaite'? If so, point out that their ancestors may have come from a place of that name, which may have had Viking origins. Explain how people were often called Roger of Braithwaite, for example, if they came from that place. This was then later contracted into Roger Braithwaite.

## Main teaching activity

● Look at a map of Britain and find where the Vikings settled. This was largely in the north and in East Anglia.
● Discuss with the whole class the significance of place names as an historical source and how they help us to understand more about people in the past.
● Create a role play where children take on the roles of Viking chiefs and elders who are working out new names for their area. Give the children a list of names describing particular places, which need to be written in a Viking style, for example, 'church village' (kirkby), 'grassy clearing' (grassthwaite), and so on. In their roles, the elders can discuss why they are giving places those names.
● Ask the children to think of special places they know of and try to work out Viking endings for their names. They can use a computer to cut and paste name endings.

## Plenary

● Review the ideas the children have had for new Viking names.

## Differentiation

Differentiate support for children in the working out of Viking name endings. More able children could look at the map of Britain and see if they can spot any other places with Viking names.

## Links
NLS Y3 Word level work: vocabulary extension by collecting new words from reading and work in other subjects;
NLS Y3 T2 Word 12: to generate compound words.
NLS Y3 T2 Text 17: to make clear notes.
NC Geography KS2: (2c) to use globes and maps.
NC ICT KS2: (2a) to develop and refine ideas by reorganising text.

© The Drawing Room

# Map of invaders and settlers

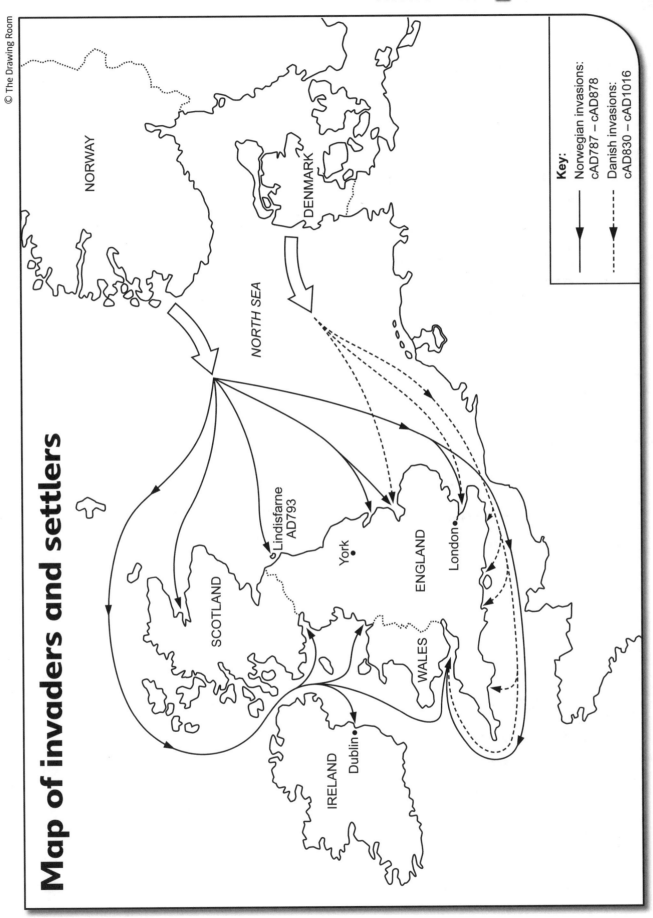

**Key:**

Norwegian invasions:
cAD787 – cAD878

Danish invasions:
cAD830 – cAD1016

NORWAY

DENMARK

NORTH SEA

Lindisfarne
AD793

York

ENGLAND

London

SCOTLAND

WALES

IRELAND

Dublin

# Event cards

| 55BC The first arrival of the Romans under the leadership of Julius Caesar. They did not stay in Britain this time. | AD43 The invasion of Britain by the Romans under their general Claudius. |
|---|---|
| AD446 The Saxons begin to arrive in Britain after the Romans have gone. | AD780 onwards Offa's Dyke. Built by the Saxon King, Offa, to defend his country against the Celts in Wales. |
| AD878 The treaty between King Alfred and Guthrum the Dane. | AD1016 Peace made between the Danes and the Saxons by King Canute. |

# Queen Boudicca

For a long time after their invasion of Britain, the Romans were not popular and they were constantly under attack from the Ancient British tribes. The most serious was the revolt in AD60, when tribes in eastern Britain massacred the inhabitants of several towns and one army legion of nearly 6000 soldiers. The uprising was led by Boudicca, the queen of the Iceni tribe.

The trouble began following the death of an important British king. Prasutagus, King of the Iceni, had become very wealthy during the course of his long reign. Before he died, he made a will, in which he left half of his wealth to his two daughters and the other half to the Roman Emperor, hoping that this would avoid trouble between them. Soon after he died however, the Romans began to divide his lands and property among themselves. Queen Boudicca was publicly whipped and her daughters badly treated. Leaders in the area had their wealth and positions seized, while the king's relatives were made slaves. Very quickly the local tribes were alienated. Uprising and revolt spread quickly to the neighbouring tribe of the Trinovantes. Many of the tribes in the south joined Boudicca, who wanted revenge for the disgraceful way she and her family and kinsmen had been treated. At first her forces were successful, as they burned and killed the inhabitants of Colchester and then swept through the countryside, eventually burning to the ground the new Roman port of Londinium.

Greatly alarmed, the Romans gathered an army and fought Boudicca somewhere in the Midlands. The slaughter was terrible. It was said that 80,000 Britons died and 70,000 on the Roman side, including those Britons who supported them. The Britons were defeated and it is said that Boudicca poisoned herself. The Romans then conducted a merciless wasting by fire and the sword of any remaining rebels.

# Celtic and Roman ways of life compared

| Roman way of life | Celtic way of life |
|---|---|
| Like to live in towns in villas which are cool and airy | Live in small villages in round huts with straw roofs |
| Build large farms | Live in hill forts behind steep ramparts |
| Like to go to the baths every day if they live in town, have feasts and drink wine | Like to play music, sing, recite poetry and make jewellery |
| Like to meet and discuss things in the Forum | The chieftains hold meetings in their large huts |
| Men can vote but women cannot vote | Tribes are ruled by a chief and nobles |
| Worship many ancient gods | Druidism is their religion |
| Boys go to school and girls work in the house with their mothers | Boys and girls work on the farms with their parents |
| Speak Latin | Speak Celtic languages |
| Write and make books | Do not write or have books, but like to tell stories and talk about their history |

I have also found out:

_____

_____

_____

■ S C H O L A S T I C

# The Viking raid on Lindisfarne

The morning of 8 June 793 began peacefully on the island of Lindisfarne, just like any other. The monks were up and about, quietly praying in the beautiful chapel in the monastery of St Cuthbert. The monastery, as you know, was famous for making the lovely illuminated gospels of Lindisfarne. The monastery also contained a considerable collection of treasures in the form of gold and silver religious items. It was a truly beautiful place.

Suddenly, a frightened cry from the monastery walls shattered the tranquility. A strange sight had been spotted out at sea on the distant horizon. Many strange-looking ships were approaching the island at great speed, bristling with spears, shields and men in helmets. They looked far from friendly. As the ships drew nearer, the monks could see that they were warriors and they became overwhelmed with dread. These warriors had long, wild hair that streamed out from under their metal helmets. They had rough beards and carried huge swords and shields. Their ships were equally warlike and frightening, long and sleek, with a fierce-looking carved wolf's head at the prow. From the first moment, it was clear that they had come for a fight, and they looked as if they could not wait to start.

Soon after that first terrified shout, the ships were ashore, skilfully pulled up onto the beach. The Vikings were upon them. The poor defenceless monks, nuns and villagers were no match for the skilful Vikings. The Vikings killed anyone who got in their way, seized all the treasures they could find and then drove out the monks from their church, killing some with their swords and driving others into the sea until they drowned. They smashed whatever they found, trampling through the holy places and even killed the sheep and oxen that they saw. Once they had everything that they wanted, they took some of the poor people onto their ships to turn into slaves, and sailed away with all their booty.

Some have said that this dreadful attack was sent by God as punishment for the sins of the people of Lindisfarne. I think though that the Vikings, who lived over the great seas to the north, in the lands of ice and snow, had heard of this legendary treasure and were intent on taking it for themselves.

# Extract from the Anglo-Saxon Chronicle

## The Danes are Defeated!

*AD878*

*This year about mid-winter, after twelfth-night, the Danish army stole out to Chippenham, and rode over the land of the West-Saxons; where they settled, and drove many of the people over sea; and of the rest the greatest part they rode down, and subdued to their will; -- ALL BUT ALFRED THE KING.*

*In the Easter of this year King Alfred with his little force raised a work at Athelney; from which he assailed the army, assisted by that part of Somersetshire which was nighest to it. Then, in the seventh week after Easter, he rode to Brixton by the eastern side of Selwood; and there came out to meet him all the people of Somersetshire, and Wiltshire, and that part of Hampshire which is on this side of the sea; and they rejoiced to see him.*

*Then within one night he went from this retreat to Hey; and within one night after he proceeded to Heddington; and there fought with all the army, and put them to flight, riding after them as far as the fortress, where he remained a fortnight. Then the army gave him hostages with many oaths, that they would go out of his kingdom. They told him also, that their king would receive baptism.*

*And they acted accordingly; for in the course of three weeks after, King Guthrum, attended by some thirty of the worthiest men that were in the army, came to him at Aller, which is near Athelney, and there the king became his sponsor in baptism ... He was there twelve nights with the king, who honoured him and his attendants with many presents.*

# A story about King Alfred

The Vikings had for many years invaded and settled many parts of England. In 871 the Vikings attacked the last remaining Anglo-Saxon kingdom of Wessex. Their victory seemed certain, but the new king, Alfred, would not give in. After a surprise attack by the Vikings, almost all of the kingdom surrendered, but not Alfred. He escaped to hide in the marshes in Somerset, where he knew he could plan how to win back his kingdom. Here he was so busy thinking about his troubles that he failed to notice some loaves burning.

A famous story has been told about him ever since this time. This version of the story is the earliest one that we know of:

*There is a place in the remote parts of English Britain far to the west, which in English is called Athelney. It is surrounded on all sides by vast salt marshes with some level ground in the middle.*

*King Alfred happened to come there as a lone traveller. Noticing the cottage of a swineherd, he sought there a peaceful retreat. He was given refuge and he stayed there for a number of days. He remained there awaiting God's mercy, impoverished, subdued and content with the bare necessities.*

*Now it happened by chance one day that the king remained at home alone with the swineherd's wife. The wife had put some bread in the oven, ready for her husband's return. She was busy with her jobs on the other side of the room, when she saw the bread burning. She immediately grew angry and said to the king (unknown to her as such), "Look here, man, you did not turn the loaves which you saw burning, yet you are quite happy to eat them when they come warm from the oven."*

*Somewhat shaken by the woman's scolding, the king not only turned the bread, but even attended to them when they were ready.*

*Soon after this, Alfred led his small band across several counties, where he gained increasing support, particularly from the men of Somerset and Wiltshire. With this large army, Alfred defeated the Danes at Edington in 878. Following the defeat of the Vikings, Guthrum the Dane agreed to be baptised and to become a Christian. He also signed a peace treaty, agreeing to live in his own part of the country and not to attack the Saxons of Wessex. Alfred's reign was, from then on, a peaceful one.*

# Tudor times

This chapter highlights three aspects of this period. The first is the different ways of life of the rich and poor in Tudor times. The teaching of this period often concentrates on the lives of the monarchs and the aristocracy. This chapter gives equal weight to both rich and poor people and introduces children to examples of Tudor woodcuts, which show the less attractive side of life in Tudor times. The second aspect is 'the wives of Henry VIII and his reasons for marrying six times'. This is a complex issue for young children and the focus in this chapter is therefore on investigation of sources. Finally, the voyages of exploration are considered, with special attention paid to Francis Drake and Walter Raleigh. Globes, maps and stories are introduced to support understanding of the distances and places that were explored, and the conditions experienced.

| | OBJECTIVES | MAIN ACTIVITY |
|---|---|---|
| **Lesson 1** | To ask and answer questions, and to select and record information. | Children look at pictures of rich and poor people in Tudor times. |
| **Lesson 2** | To ask and answer questions, and record information.<br>To know about characteristic features of the period studied. | In pairs, children search sources to find answers to their questions about rich and poor people in Tudor times. |
| **Lesson 3** P | To find out about the past from pictures.<br>To recall, select and organise historical information. | Looking at how the Tudors dressed, children sort pictures into two sets, one showing the rich and one the poor and then 'clothe' an image appropriately. |
| **Lesson 4** | To find out about the past from historic sites.<br>To ask and answer questions, and record information. | Children visit an historical site or use the internet to learn about Tudor houses. |
| **Lesson 5** P | To find out about the past from written sources. | A will and an inventory provide two different sources for children to investigate lifestyles of the rich and poor. |
| **Lesson 6** P | To find out about the past from pictures.<br>To recognise that the past is represented and interpreted in different ways. | Children examine woodcuts to learn about how the poor were treated in Tudor times. |
| **Lesson 7** | To recognise that the past is represented and interpreted in different ways.<br>To find out about the past from portraits. | Children look carefully at portraits and write a short descriptive paragraph about the person in a selected painting. |
| **Lesson 8** | To recognise that the past is represented and interpreted in different ways.<br>To find out about the past from a variety of sources. | Children try to chronologically order paintings of Henry VIII at different stages in his life. They then create their own sequence of pictures. |
| **Lesson 9** | To recognise that the past is represented and interpreted in different ways.<br>To recall, select and organise historical information. | In groups, children research one of the wives of Henry VIII and together create a chart showing all his wives. |
| **Lesson 10** | To place events, periods and changes into correct periods of time.<br>To identify and describe reasons for historical events. | Children consider the different reasons why Henry VIII married his six wives. |
| **Lesson 11** P | To find out about the past from maps, globes and a range of historical sources.<br>To communicate their knowledge in a variety of ways. | Children learn about Tudor exploration and create scenes about life on board a Tudor ship. |
| **Lesson 12** P | To find out about the past from story. | In groups, children investigate the stories of Drake and Raleigh and create short playscripts. |
| **Lesson 13** | To place events, people and changes into correct periods of time.<br>To use dates and vocabulary relating to the passing of time.<br>To recall, select and organise historical information. | Children create a whole-class timeline of the Tudor period. |

**100 HISTORY LESSONS: Ages 7-11**

# Finding out about the rich and poor in Tudor times

## Objectives
● To ask and answer questions, and to select and record information relevant to the focus of the enquiry.

## Vocabulary
sources, information, enquire

## Resources
Two pictures from Tudor times - one showing the rich, the other the poor. For example use websites like www.englishhistory.net/tudor.html and www.spartacus.schoolnet.co.uk/TUDpoverty.htm; pens and paper.

## Links
NLS Y3 T1 Sentence 6: to secure knowledge of question marks and use appropriately in their own writing.
NLS Y3 T2 Text 17: to make clear notes.
NC English KS2: En1 (3) to talk effectively as members of a group.

## Background
The general opinion of the age was that if you were very poor but able-bodied then your poverty must be your own fault. A second group of poor, the deserving poor, included those who fell ill, lost their employment, or were wounded during warfare. These people often suffered considerable hardship, to the point of starvation. Monasteries were the only refuge for those in severe difficulties. In addition, there were servants, labourers, craftspeople and peasants working on the land, who were poor but just able to make a living. At the same time, the number of rich people was growing. There was an expansion of the middle classes, particularly people such as merchants, whose businesses were developing rapidly at this time. The nobility and monarchy were the richest of all, living on inherited wealth, property and lands.

## Introduction
● Talk about how today there are some people who are very rich and some who do not have much money. Give examples and prompt the children to think of some, such as: the Queen and David and Victoria Beckham. Examples of poorer people might include poor pensioners, homeless people or refugees. (It is important to remember that these issues need to be treated sensitively, since some children in the class may be personally affected by them).
● Discuss how we know about rich and poor people. Ask the children what sources we could use today, such as newspapers, the internet or television. How might they find out about people in Tudor times?

## Main teaching activity
● Display two contrasting pictures of people in Tudor times - one showing rich people and one showing the poor. Ask the children to comment on what they can see.
● Ask the children to work in pairs to discuss what they would like to know about the rich and poor in Tudor times, such as what sort of lives they led, what sort of work they did and why they were poor.
● Ask the children, in pairs, to write a list of their questions and to suggest ideas about where they might find some answers. What sources could they use?

## Plenary
● Share ideas and compile a list of class questions that the children would like to find the answers to. (These can be used in Lesson 2.)

## Differentiation
Mixed ability pairs will provide support for the less able children.

# Using evidence about rich and the poor in Tudor times

## Objectives
● To ask and answer questions, and to select and record information relevant to the focus of the enquiry.
● To know about characteristic features of the period studied.
● To find out about the events, people and changes studied from an appropriate range of sources of information.

## Vocabulary
portrait, woodcut, will

## Resources
List of questions from Lesson 1 (if possible); selection of pictures, modern and contemporary, and written sources, including websites, such as www.historylearning site.co.uk/ and www.schoolhistory.co.uk/ primarylinks/Tudortimes; paper, pens and pencils.

## Links
NLS Y3 T2 Text 17: to make clear notes.
NC English KS2: En1 (3) to talk effectively as members of a group.

## Background
There is a vast amount of visual and written information you can use for this lesson. Probably the most easily accessible sources are pictures, in the form of modern-day illustrations of both rich and poor people from textbooks, primary information books and the internet, contemporary Tudor woodcuts showing the poor and also portraits made by artists at the time, commissioned by the rich.

Written sources include inventories made following the death of a poor person and wills made by the rich, who could afford somebody to draw up a will for them.

## Introduction
● Explain the lesson objectives to the class.
● Remind the children of the list of questions they made in Lesson 1. Display the list clearly for the children to see. If this is not possible, ask general questions, such as: *How can we find out about the rich and the poor? What would we like to know?*
● Tell the children that they are going to investigate and find out some answers to their questions using different sources.

## Main teaching activity
● Provide the class with a range of sources. These might include: woodcuts of poor people, portraits and paintings of the rich, illustrations from information books, photographs of stately homes, written accounts and so on.
● Discuss how the children need to look carefully at their sources, and ask and answer questions about them.
● Organise the children to work in pairs and give each pair one or more of the questions to try to answer.
● Guide the pairs to look at relevant sources in order to answer their questions and to make brief notes of their answers.

## Plenary
● Invite each pair to share their answers with the rest of the class.
● Ask each pair to choose one source that they have used, and to create their own drawings, in pencil or pen and ink, of either a rich or poor person in Tudor times.

## Differentiation
Organise the class to work in mixed ability pairs to provide support for the less able children. Provide a framework for the questions and answers for the less able children, perhaps including sentence starters for the answers. More able children should be encouraged to research their sources in more depth.

# Dressing the rich and poor

## Objectives
● To find out about the events, people and changes studied from pictures.
● To recall, select and organise historical information.

## Vocabulary
gown, coat, cloak

## Resources
The photocopiable sheet 'Dress a rich or poor Tudor boy' on page 40, one per child; scissors (child use); paper and colouring materials; selection of pictures of rich and poor people in Tudor times, showing the type of dress they wore (useful websites include http://atschool.eduweb.co.uk/nettsch/time/tudors.html and www.bbc.co.uk/history/games/costumes).

## Background
A common visual impression of Tudor times is one of people dressed in elaborate clothes made from expensive fabrics, such as velvet and silk, finely decorated and adorned with jewels. This is the view of Tudor times that we have from seeing portraits of the rich. However, the majority of people would have been quite simply, or even poorly dressed. The poor would have worn clothes that looked dull by comparison, since bright colours required expensive dyes, making the cloth itself very expensive. The fabrics would also have been cheaper and locally made from wool, linen or leather. Neither rich nor poor paid much attention to cleanliness and clothes would rarely have been washed.

## Introduction
● Introduce the children to the lesson objectives and ask questions such as: *How can we tell the difference between rich and poor people in Tudor times?*
● Explain that they will be using the information they find from pictures to make their own picture of a rich or poor person.

## Main teaching activity
● Ask the children to sort the pictures into two sets, one showing the rich and one showing the poor. Encourage the children to make comparisons between the two sets of pictures.
● Discuss what the main differences are between the types of clothes worn.
● Look at the photocopiable sheet 'Dress a rich or poor Tudor boy' on page 40 with the class and discuss which clothes would be worn by both a rich and a poor person.
● Give a copy of the sheet to each child and ask them to cut out the clothes, sort them into those suitable for either rich or poor, and then use them to 'dress' the figure on their sheet. They will need to select appropriate dress for either a rich or a poor person.
● As an extension to this, children could research and draw women and children dressed appropriately.

## Plenary
● Ask the children to come out in turn with the figures they have dressed and make a wall display or place them on a background to create, for example, a Tudor street scene.

## Links
NC Design and technology KS2: (2d) to cut and shape a range of materials, and assemble materials accurately.

## Differentiation
Provide additional adult support for any children with fine motor difficulties or other special needs during the cutting out of the figures and clothes. Encourage more able children to make a list of the types of clothing worn by Tudor people.

# Tudor buildings

## Background
The activities suggested for this lesson could be carried out during a visit to an historical site or by using information on the internet. If you are planning a visit, then make a 'pre-visit' to the site to identify key teaching points and to find out about the facilities available to the children. Consider key questions to ask the children, prepare sketching and note-making materials and carry out a risk assessment. Organise and meet a small team of helpers, such as parents, carers and extra staff to discuss the visit. Provide them with brief notes about your objectives, the main activities of the day, and their role during the visit. (These notes could be sent to helpers if a meeting is not possible.)

## Introduction
● Explain the lesson objectives to the class and together prepare a list of relevant questions to answer.
● If you are planning a visit, remind the children of good behaviour and staying in their groups.

## Main teaching activity
● During the investigation or visit, ask the children to organise their observations to answer the questions they have previously suggested, such as: *How big were rooms in Tudor houses? What was the style of doors and windows? How were things different from modern buildings, such as the chimneys? What did Tudor rooms look like? What kind of furniture did they have?*
● Encourage the children to note the details in Tudor buildings, such as the pattern of the brickwork, the use of carving in stone and woodwork.
● Following the visit or website investigation, ask the children to review their observations and use them to answer questions, such as: *What building materials did the Tudors use and why? Why were their windows small? Why did they make such large chimneys? How much furniture did they have? What was it made from and why? What sort of things did the Tudors not have that we have today?*

## Plenary
● Provide drawing materials and challenge the children to make a sketch of some details found in the Tudor house or building, including the features they have learned about, such as patterns of brickwork, ceiling designs, doors and so on.

## Differentiation
Organise the class to work in mixed ability groups or pairs to provide support for the less able children. If available, some children may find it easier to use a digital camera to record features while on the visit.

# Inventories and wills

## Objectives
● To find out about the events, people and changes studied from written sources.

## Vocabulary
inventory, possessions, belongings

## Resources
The photocopiable sheets 'A Tudor will' and 'A Tudor inventory' on pages 41 and 42, one per child.

## Links
NLS Y3 Word level work: vocabulary extension by collecting new words from reading and work in other subjects.
NLS Y3 T2 Text 17: to make clear notes.

## Background
Both wills and inventories were common in Tudor times. Wills were left by the more wealthy, who had an understanding of their significance and who could pay for a will-writer or lawyer to prepare one for them. Poor people, of course, could neither read nor had the money for such a service. Their possessions were therefore simply listed in the form of an inventory, ready for disposal after their death. Both types of document serve as very useful sources for highlighting the great differences between the possessions of the rich compared with the very little owned by the poor.

## Introduction
● Explain the lesson objectives to the class and tell them that they are going to look at written sources in this lesson.
● Ask if anyone has ever heard of a person leaving a will when they have died. Explain the purpose of a will.
● Discuss how the Tudors had wills and also inventories. Explain what an inventory was.
● Ask questions such as: *Why did the Tudors use both wills and inventories? How are they different?*

## Main teaching activity
● Give each child copies of the photocopiable sheets 'A Tudor will' and 'A Tudor inventory' on pages 41 and 42.
● Read through the will and the inventory with the class as a shared reading session and provide support where necessary with unfamiliar vocabulary and spellings.
● Without explaining who they were written for, ask the children questions such as: *What kind of person was this made for? What did they own? What does this tell us about the person?*
● Focus on the differences between the will and the inventory and also any similarities.
● Set the children the task, to be completed at home if necessary, of making an inventory of all the things in their bedroom, to compare with the inventory they have seen. (You will need to be sensitive to individual children's circumstances and, if more appropriate, ask the children to create an inventory of items in the classroom.)

## Plenary
● Review the children's findings about wills and inventories. Clarify any misconceptions they may have and compare their own inventories with the Tudor one, discussing the main differences and similarities.

## Differentiation
Provide additional support for the less able and encourage the more able to use descriptive words and adjectives when writing inventories.

🔲 **31**

# What happened to the poor in Tudor times?

## Objectives
● To find out about the events, people and changes studied from pictures.
● To recognise that the past is represented and interpreted in different ways.

## Vocabulary
starve, poverty, punishment

## Resources
The photocopiable sheet 'Tudor woodcuts' on page 43, one per child and one of the illustrations enlarged for class work; for more examples of tudor woodcuts showing the poor see www.bvt.org.uk/sellymanor/tudors.html

## Background
Woodcuts were widely made during Tudor times, using the block printing method, with the pictures simply carved onto wooden blocks. They are a very valuable source for studying the period because they often contain pictures portraying a totally different side of life compared with the portraits and scenes painted for the rich. Woodcuts sometimes reveal extreme poverty and they provide a different interpretation of what life was like, and were intended to make this point. To neglect these images would indeed result in children gaining a very one-sided view of Tudor life.

## Introduction
● Discuss what happens if someone is very poor today, either in this country or in another one, for example, there may be help and money for them to buy food. Say that money is raised from taxes to pay for this. If they live in a poor part of the world, they may have food provided for them. Explain how this is raised mostly by charities and by governments.
● Talk about the lesson objective and tell the class that some information about what happened to the poor in Tudor times can be found from pictures that were made at the time.

## Main teaching activity
● Show the children the woodcuts showing scenes from the lives of the poor and punishments for the poor, using the photocopiable sheet 'Tudor woodcuts' on page 43.
● Use one of the illustrations enlarged to demonstrate to the class how to interpret the source. Model some questions that they could ask, such as: *How was this picture made? What sort of people does it show? How are they dressed? What is happening in the picture?*
● Discuss why the woodcut was made and whether the artist wanted to show these things. Compare them to oil paintings that depict the rich and discuss the different materials that were used to make them.
● Ask children to work in pairs to discuss what the sources tell them.
● Then ask them to work with their partners to create freeze frames or mimes representing the scenes they have looked at.

## Plenary
● Invite the pairs in turn to perform their freeze frames and mimes to the class. The children should try to guess what is happening.

## Differentiation
Organise the class to work in mixed ability groups or pairs to provide support for the less able children.

# How do we know about the rich in Tudor times?

## Background
Portraits are both an excellent source of information on Tudor times, and also a useful type of stimulus for developing children's historical skills. They provide the opportunity for informed enquiry through the process of asking and answering questions - important skills in interrogating sources. They also provide an opportunity to discuss the notion of historical interpretation, since each portrait we see is the interpretation of the age by that particular artist.

## Introduction
● Ask the class: *What do portraits tell us about the rich in Tudor times?*
● Discuss what a portrait is (that is: a painting or drawing made of a person by an artist as a record of what they looked like).

## Main teaching activity
● Provide copies of a variety of Tudor portraits, one for each child in the class.
● Look at one enlarged portrait together with the class, for example, a portrait of Queen Elizabeth I.
● Model how to ask questions about what the portrait shows us about the person, for example, the status of the person, their wealth, their character. Ask the children: *Why was the portrait made?* (For example, to show the wealth and power of the person in it or as a family record).
● Let the children work on their portraits in pairs. Challenge them to think of questions about their portraits and then to try to answer them from making observations and inferences about the portraits. For example, a person might look very haughty or stern, and this might indicate how important they were and what they were like as a person.
● Encourage the children to write a short descriptive paragraph about the person in their portrait.

## Plenary
● Display the tudor portraits alongside the children's written work. Invite individuals to read out their paragraphs to the rest of the class as they view the portraits.

## Differentiation
Organise the class to work in mixed ability pairs to provide support for the less able children. Encourage more able writers to compose a longer paragraph about their portrait. Provide a framework to enable less able writers to complete their piece of writing.

## Objectives
● To ask and answer questions, and to select and record information relevant to the focus of the enquiry.
● To recognise that the past is represented and interpreted in different ways.
● To find out about the events, people and changes studied from portraits.

## Vocabulary
portrait, painting, wealth, status

## Resources
Selection of portraits of prominent people from Tudor times, one enlarged for class work (useful information and resources can be found in picture packs such as those produced by PCET (www.pcet.co.uk) and on websites such as the National Portrait Gallery site: www.npg.org.uk/live/second.asp); art materials and paper.

## Links
NLS Y3-4 Text level work: writing composition by writing portraits of characters and character sketches.
NC English KS2: En1 (3) to talk effectively as members of a group.

# Sources about Henry VIII

## Objectives
● To recognise that the past is represented and interpreted in different ways.
● To find out about the events, people and changes studied from an appropriate range of sources of information.

## Vocabulary
sequence, ageing, changing

## Resources
Three, four or five portraits showing Henry VIII at different times in his life, one set of each per group of children (there are a number of portraits shown on www.marileecody.com/henry8images.html); art materials and drawing paper.

## Links
NC Art and design KS2: (1a) to record from experience and imagination, to select and record from first-hand observation and to explore ideas for different purposes.
NC English KS2: En1 (3) to talk effectively as members of a group.

### Background
Henry VIII changed a great deal over the course of his life. He was a very intelligent child, quick to learn, and a good musician and sportsman. He loved riding and jousting as a young man, and earned a reputation as one of the most eligible princes in Europe. He was tall and very good-looking according to Tudor fashion. However, as Henry grew older, he began to overeat, and suffered from many serious illnesses, mostly self-imposed. These all caused him to gradually become the very obese and ugly character that we see portrayed in paintings made during the last years of his life.

### Introduction
● Talk with the class about Henry VIII. Ask who has heard of him before and what they know about him already.
● Explain that they are now going to look at some of the portraits that were made of Henry VIII during his life, and they are going to try to answer the question: *What do the portraits tell us about Henry VIII?*

### Main teaching activity
● Organise the children to work in small groups and provide each with a set of portraits showing Henry at different stages in his life.
● Ask the children to look closely at each one and then to try to order them chronologically. Encourage the children to look for clues to help them judge which portrait should come first, second and so on.
● After a suitable time, work together as a class to order the portraits correctly. Encourage the children to give the reasons for their decisions.
● Provide art materials and paper for the children to make their own sequence of pictures, showing how Henry changed and aged over time.
● Make a display of the children's pictures, alongside a set of the portraits discussed at the beginning of the lesson.

### Plenary
● Discuss how the portraits show us how Henry changed and tell us something about his life. In particular, ask the children to look for clues about his personality, physical health and wealth.

### Differentiation
Provide additional adult support for any children with fine motor difficulties or other special needs during the art task. More able children could be asked to write captions or sentences to go with the pictures in the display.

# The six wives of Henry VIII

## Objectives
- To recognise that the past is represented and interpreted in different ways.
- To find out about the events, people and changes studied from an appropriate range of sources of information.
- To recall, select and organise historical information.

## Vocabulary
wife, wives, marry, marriage

## Resources
Pictures, portraits, books, resource packs and appropriate websites relating to Henry VIII and his wives, such as www.englishhistory.net/tudor/monarchs/wives.html

## Links
NLS Y4 T2 Text 23: to collect information from a variety of sources and present it in one simple format.
NC Art and design KS2: (2c) to use a variety of methods and approaches to communicate observations, ideas and feelings.
NC ICT KS2: (1a) to talk about what information they need and how they can find and use it.

## Background
Henry VIII married six wives: Catherine of Aragon, Anne Boleyn, Jane Seymour, Anne of Cleves, Catherine Howard and Katherine Parr. Catherine of Aragon was a Spanish princess, some years older than Henry; she had already been married to Henry's older brother, Arthur. The marriage had been a political arrangement made by Henry's father, Henry VII. Henry VIII next married Anne Boleyn, partly because of his need for a male heir, which Catherine had not been able to provide, and also for love. Similarly Jane Seymour and Catherine Howard were marriages that arose from Henry's notorious affairs with young ladies at the court, all ending unhappily. Henry married Anne of Cleves, from the West German duchy of Cleve, in order, once again, to build a political ally, this time in his fight against the Catholic states.

However, Anne did not like him and he thought she was ugly, not at all like the picture he had seen of her before the marriage. He is said by many to have married Katherine Parr, who had already been married twice before, largely so that she could nurse him in his old age and ill-health. Whether this was indeed his purpose or not, this was, in fact, what Katherine's role was until Henry's death in 1547.

## Introduction
- Ask the class: *Who were Henry VIII's six wives?*
- Find out what the children already know and explain that they are now going to investigate further and find out more about Henry's six wives.

## Main teaching activity
- Divide the class into six groups and ask each group to research one of Henry's wives. They need to find out who she was and what she was like.
- Provide each group with a range of sources, such as pictures, portraits, books, resource packs and appropriate websites.
- Give the children materials to produce a chart about each wife for display. Suggest that they include at least two or three pictures and some notes about their chosen wife, organised under headings such as: Country of birth; A royal background; Married for love; Married for political reasons, and so on.

## Plenary
- Arrange the children's charts in a wall display, in chronological order, according to the order that Henry married each wife.

## Differentiation
Organise the class to work in mixed ability groups to provide support for the less able children.

# Henry's reasons for marrying six wives

## Background

There were a number of reasons for Henry VIII marrying so many times. The most obvious one was the need for a male heir to maintain the Tudor succession. Henry divorced Catherine of Aragon since she was believed to be too old to bear a son, and Anne Boleyn was already pregnant with Elizabeth. Henry also married for political reasons. A good marriage could confirm an alliance with a foreign power, as in the case of Henry's first marriage to a Spanish princess and then to Anne of Cleves, a member of a ruling protestant family.

Henry also married for love - notably in his marriages to Anne Boleyn, Jane Seymour and Catherine Howard. His marriage to Anne Boleyn led to the split with the Roman Catholic Church and the setting up of the Church of England, with Henry as its head. Jane Seymour, believed by some historians to be Henry's true love, died in childbirth. Finally, Henry married for convenience. It is thought that he married Katherine Parr so that she would nurse him through the ill-health of his old age. Katherine Parr outlived him.

## Introduction
● Explain how Henry VIII married six different wives during his reign.
● Tell the class that in this lesson, they are going to investigate why this was, and try to answer the question: *Why did Henry VIII marry six times?*

## Main teaching activity
● Briefly tell the children the stories of the six wives.
● Tell the children the rhyme about Henry's wives and give them time to rehearse and recite it themselves: *Divorced, beheaded, died Divorced, beheaded, survived*.
● Use maps to find where each of Henry's foreign wives came from and discuss how many had come from another country. Ask the children why they think this was.
● Talk about Henry's different reasons for marrying wives who did not come from abroad.
● Divide the class into six groups to research into each wife in order to explain the lines about them in the rhyme.
● Talk about what happened to Henry and his children in the end.

## Plenary
● Use a large class timeline and some portraits to illustrate the key events in the family life of Henry VIII.

## Differentiation
Mixed ability groups will provide support for the less able children.

# Exploration in Tudor times

## Objectives
● To find out about the events, people and changes studied from maps, globes and a range of historical sources.
● To communicate their knowledge and understanding of history in a variety of ways.

## Vocabulary
explorer, exploration, voyage

## Resources
The photocopiable sheet 'Life on board ship' on page 44; maps or globes of the world; pictures and written descriptions of sea voyages, for example, from the National Maritime Museum, and websites, such as www.nmm.ac.uk/ TudorExploration/ NMMFLASH/index.htm and www.woodlands-junior. kent.sch.uk/Homework/ tudors/exploration.htm

## Links
NC English KS2: En1 (4a) to create, adapt and sustain different roles, individually and in groups. NC Geography KS2: (2c) to use atlases and globes, and maps and plans at a range of scales.

## Background
The Tudor period was an important time for exploration and world travel. Along with breakthroughs in other areas of knowledge, the use of maps and skills in ship building and navigation developed rapidly during the period. With these new skills, tools and knowledge, men from Europe began to venture further afield into Africa, Asia and the new world of America. Adventurers from Britain were among these explorers and included famous men such as: Francis Drake, Walter Raleigh, John Hawkins, John Cabot and Martin Frobisher.

## Introduction
● Explain to the class that in this lesson they are going to think about the following questions: *Where did the Tudors travel to? How did they get there?*

## Main teaching activity
● Using a globe, point out the places visited in Tudor times. Discuss where these places are, and how the Tudors got to them.
● Look at pictures of Tudor ships and use the photocopiable sheet 'Life on board ship' on page 44 to talk about what it must have been like to undertake such long voyages on ships like these - cramped conditions, dangers of piracy, lack of fresh food and water and sailors' superstitions and fears of things such as sea monsters.
● Discuss how the sailors coped with these problems.
● In groups, ask the children to create short dramatic scenes about life on board a Tudor ship. They could be scenes about: a lack of water to drink; weevils in the food; sea monsters sighted nearby; violent storms; hot, stifling weather.
● Alternatively, ask the children to write a short, first-person narrative, describing what it was like on board a Tudor ship, facing the excitement, fear and loneliness of the journey.

## Plenary
● Provide an opportunity for each group to share their scenes with the class, or for individual children to read out their narratives.
● Consider the differences between travel these days and during Tudor times. Emphasise that these days we have comfortable travel, including aeroplanes and cars and that journeys are much quicker and that we often know what to expect at our destination.

## Differentiation
Less able children may require extra time looking at the globe or map to understand the journeys the explorers made. Encourage more able children to locate relevant locations on the globe. Provide additional adult support for any children with writing difficulties or other special needs during the writing task.

# Drake and Raleigh

## Objectives
● To find out about the events, people and changes studied from story.

## Vocabulary
adventure, famous, traveller

## Resources
The photocopiable sheet 'An account of the life of Sir Walter Raleigh by a friend' and 'An account of Sir Francis Drake's life by a friend' on page 45; highlighter pens or coloured pencils.

## Links
NC English KS2: En1 (4a) to create, adapt and sustain different roles, individually and in groups.

## Background
Drake and Raleigh are perhaps two of the better known of the explorers from the British Isles. Not necessarily setting out with discovery as their main purpose, the two men engaged in commercial activities, piracy and warfare, as well as helping to chart new parts of the globe. Drake is especially remembered for his circumnavigation of the world and for his lucrative attacks against the Spanish treasure fleets, while Raleigh is remembered for his adventures in America, bringing back items such as tobacco and potatoes to Britain for the first time, and also his attempts to set up a new 'City of Raleigh' in America.

## Introduction
● Ask the class who has heard of Francis Drake or Walter Raleigh. Ask if they know why these men are famous.
● Explain that they were famous explorers and adventurers in Tudor times, along with several others, such as Hawkins, Frobisher and Cabot.
● Say that in this lesson they are going to find out more about Drake and Raleigh, and try to answer the question: *How can we retell the stories of Drake and Raleigh?*

## Main teaching activity
● Divide the class into two and give one half copies of the account about Sir Francis Drake the other half the account of Sir Walter Raleigh, using photocopiable page 45.
● Ask the children to read their account and, working in smaller groups, to highlight the key events in their story.
● Set each small group the task of writing a short playscript of a scene showing one of the key events in their account. Try to make sure that all the major happenings are covered, rather than the same scene being retold by each group.
● Ask the children to perform their scenes in sequence to retell each famous man's story to the other half of the class.

## Plenary
● Make a small display of the accounts, playscripts and pictures of the two explorers, and maps showing the routes of their journeys.
● Ask the children to compare the two explorers and their achievements. What is similar or different about them?

## Differentiation
Organise the class to work in mixed ability groups or pairs to provide support for the less able. More able children will be able to work independently to create their scenes. Use extra adult help to ensure all the children take part in writing and performing a scene.

# Making a Tudor timeline

## Objectives
● To place events, people and changes into correct periods of time.
● To use dates and vocabulary relating to the passing of time.
● To recall, select and organise historical information.

## Vocabulary
sequence, timeline, chronological order

## Resources
Large blank timeline containing the dates at the beginning and end of the Tudor period; blank event cards; pictures, portraits, books, resource packs and appropriate websites on the Tudors.

## Links
NLS Y3 T2 Text 17: to make clear notes; Y4 T2 Text 23: to collect information from a variety of sources and present it in one simple format.
NC ICT S2: (1a) to talk about what information they need and how they can find and use it.

## Background
Children find time and chronology one of the most difficult concepts to grasp. It is important, therefore, to provide them with as many varied opportunities as possible to develop a good understanding. By this stage in their learning, some children will be beginning to comprehend the significance of dates, but they are still likely to need considerable support in using dates on a timeline and in ordering events chronologically. For this reason, the assembling of information on the class timeline is suggested as a whole-class activity, where the teacher can observe, prompt and support children in their attempts to sort and sequence what they have learned about Tudor times. Timeline activities are an ideal way of drawing together and consolidating all of the information learned about a topic.

## Introduction
● Explain to the children that the aim of this lesson is to create a large class timeline showing some of the key events of Tudor times.
● Prompt the children to recall what they have learned and found out with questions such as: What have we found out about the Tudors? Can we put what we know into the right order on a timeline?

## Main teaching activity
● Provide the children with a large blank class timeline, mounted on a suitable space on the wall where they can use it to add information.
● Organise the children to work in small groups or pairs to discuss what they have learned and can remember.
● Ask the children to make sets of cards from the work they have completed on the Tudors over the course of the topic and to carry out further research. Each group could choose a theme, such as Tudor marriages, the dates of each reign, or voyages of exploration.
● Support the groups as necessary to make sure the children are clear as to dates and the order of events, and clarify any misunderstandings or misconceptions.
● The cards should contain brief details about a person or event and relevant dates.
● As an extension activity for quicker children, illustrations could be made or printed out for the timeline.

## Plenary
● Ask each group to put their cards in the right places on the timeline. This activity can be used for assessment, if each child is then asked to individually produce a set of cards for their own timeline.

## Differentiation
Organise the class to work in mixed ability groups or pairs to provide support for the less able children.

# Dress a rich or poor Tudor boy

Cut out the outline figure and then choose a suitable set of clothes to make either a rich or a poor boy from Tudor times.

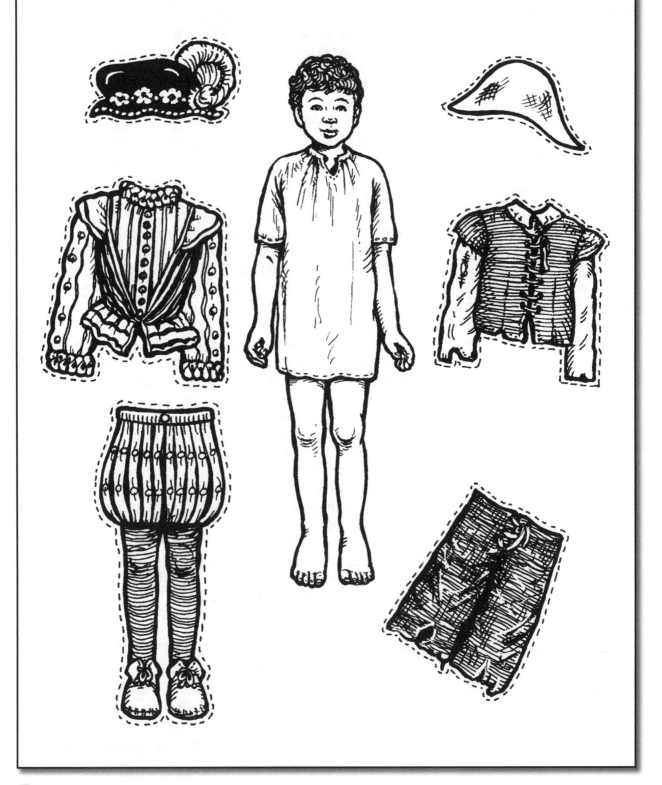

◼SCHOLASTIC

# A Tudor will and inventory

*VRSULA WOOTTON. 18 July 1553. To be buried within the quyer of the parishe churche of Bocton Malherbe yf I dy wt in that parishe or in that parish church where I shall happen to dye. For the brekinge of the grouwnd for my grave and for other things vsually demaunded by the parsones at and for suche buryalls 20s. Next my debts due to euerye person be paide. Also I will to Twentie poore men twentie shertes and to as manye wemmen twentie smokes and to eury one 12d. in mony.*

*To my sonne Thomas Wotton my Ringe with the poynted dyamonde and to my doughter Wotton my Ringe with the Rewbye and my gowne of blake veluet which she will.*

*To my sonne Rudstone the two gylte saltes that he has of myne and to my doughter Rudstone a tabylclothe of damaske work and a Towell and a dowsyn of Napkyns and a gowne of black veluet. To my saide sonne Rudston £10 he owithe me.*

*To Willyam Wotton my Ringe wt the dyamonde squared at the cornares. To Mystris Wallwicke my gowne of blacke damask that is lyned and a ringe with a Turkes.*

*To euery one of the seruauntes takinge wages being in my sonne Thomas Wottons house or els where yt shall happen me to decease 3s. 4d. and to the women 5s. apece.*

*To Sexton 40s. To Buckeman 20s. And wher as there is yet due vnto me £200 by my sonne Wotton I will give and bequeath aswell the said £200 as all the rest of my goodes &e vnto my daughter Hedyngton to be employed and bestowed within xij monethes vpon some portion of lande to be assured vnto my said daughter Hedyngton and her heiress.*

*Executours my sone Robert Rudstone and Willyam Wotton – Vrsula Wotton – Proved (before D & C Caunterbury sede vacant) 7 June 1554 by William Wotton personally and Robert Rudston in person of said William, the executors.*

Transcription by Leland Lewis Duncan. Courtesy of Kent Archaeological Society

# A Tudor inventory

6. *John Cotterell, 1572 [servant]*

*The trewe Inventorye of all the goodes and chattells latelye John Cotterell of*

*Appleby deceased given & presed the nynth day of Januarye Anno domini*

*1572 by Richard Walker, Rychard Baker, Rychard Wryght and Rycharde*

*Watthew inhabitants for that purpose as hereafter followeth*

*Imprimis Barlye and wheate prysed iii [?]*

*Item pease & hey with some otes in ye barne xls*

*Item seven bordes and two bedsydes xxd*

*Item certayne tymber xiis*

*Item syxe shepe xviis*

*Item in redye monye xxd*

*item one cheste xxd*

*Item one roobe & a peare of hose iiiid*

*Item fower landes in the feld sowen with wynter corne xvis*

*Item the lease of the house iiii [?]*

*Old currency:*
*d = old pence*
*12d = 1s = 1 shilling*
*20s = 1l = 1 old pound*

**Modern spelling**

barley and wheat 3l (?)

pease and hay with some oats in the barn 40s

seven boards and two bedsides 20d

certain timber 12s

six sheep 17s

in ready money 20d

one chest 20d

one robe and a pair of hose 4d

four lands in the field sown with winter corn 16s

the lease of the house 4l (?)

By permission of The Record Office for Leicestershire, Leicester and Rutland

◼SCHOLASTIC

**Tudor woodcuts**

# Life on board ship

We know from the things found on the Tudor ship *Mary Rose* what would have been eaten by the sailors. Here is an idea of some of these things: ship's biscuits, beer, salt beef, fish, butter and cheese.

For four days a week they ate meat and for three days fish.

Other provisions that would have been needed are likely to have been:

* sailcloth
* twine for mending sails
* barrels for storing the food, water, beer and wine
* cannon, cannon balls and gunpowder
* longbows, knives and swords
* tools
* logbook and charts for the captain
* navigation instruments for the captain
* pots and pans for the cook
* plates and cups for the sailors
* dinner service and glasses for the captain and officers.

They might also have taken some fresh fruit and vegetables and some live chickens and other animals.

Sailors frequently returned from long voyages with stories of frightening sea monsters that they had seen, some probably real sea creatures, which they had not seen very clearly because they were afraid of them, and others ones that they had imagined. Even so, many sailors really believed these monsters existed. Some of the pictures they drew of these monsters can be seen below.

# A friend's account of the life of Sir Walter Raleigh

1554–1618

Walter was a good friend to me when we were young. He had one brother, one sister and two half-brothers. We both came from good families and his in particular was quite noble and so he soon became a favourite of the Queen at Court. He had been off fighting for her in Ireland and, when he came back, they became great friends. One famous story I heard about him was that he spread his cloak across a puddle so that the Queen could walk across and not get her shoes wet. He soon became important at the Court because he was handsome, clever and good at dancing, writing and hunting. He was knighted and became Captain of the Guard. He helped to stop a plot to kill the Queen and, as a reward, she gave him a lot of land in Ireland. Raleigh was also made Governor of the Island of Jersey.

Being a favourite with the Queen meant that a lot of people were jealous of him though. Walter was always proud and had grand ideas and some people disliked him for this too. After he went to the New World and brought back strange things called tobacco and potatoes, his plans became even more ambitious. He wanted to set up a new colony there on Roanoke Island and once he got an idea in his head he just would not give up even though many good people were killed in the attempt. But he was loyal to the Queen. He paid for the building of the *Ark Royal*, which became the flagship of the navy and helped defeat the Spanish Armada. I know he was headstrong though and always wanted his own way. He started to behave badly at Court and eventually the Queen had him sent to the Tower of London. He was only saved by the fact that one of his ships brought back a lot of treasure captured from a Spanish ship, which he was able to give to the Queen. Another problem was that he was so angry about the Spanish that he continued to attack their ships even after peace had been agreed with King James I. The King did not like him, and again threw him into the Tower with orders that he must be beheaded for what he had done. Even though he was beheaded by the King, we still kept our respect for our friend and remembered him as one of England's many great sailors.

# An account of Sir Francis Drake's life by a friend c1544–1596

I've known Francis Drake since he was a boy. He came from a large family – I think there were twelve children. He was born near the sea in Devon, like me. When he was 22 years old he went off and joined a slave-trading voyage along with John Hawkins. You may have heard of him too? I suppose he thought he could make his fortune quickly; there's a lot of money in slaves. Anyway, 12 years later he sailed around the world in the *Golden Hind* – amazing. He was the first Englishman to do this, you know. We were really proud of him when he returned, and, of course, everyone wanted to know him then – he became quite famous too. He was even called to the court of Queen Elizabeth and was made a knight. After this we all had to call him *Sir* Francis Drake!

He became very important and rich and I didn't see him any more, but I know he came to live in Plymouth and that he couldn't stay away from the sea! I heard that he started to fight our old enemies the Spanish – must have been around 1585. People say though that he was fighting less for England and more for what he could thieve! No better than a common pirate some said. He loved to raid Spanish treasure ships and bring back the treasure for Queen Bess. When the Spanish Armada attacked, Drake sailed against the Spanish and burned their ships. He was one of the leading men in the defeat of the Armada. A few years later I heard he was ill and died during a long sea voyage, but, despite what some say, I will always think of him as one of the finest sailors in British history.

# CHAPTER 3

# The Second World War

This chapter focuses on aspects of the Second World War that would have had an impact on children: bombing and the devastation this caused; evacuation; the practical effects of rationing, and the lack of luxury items like toys and chocolate. These are all areas which today's children will find hard to imagine, and so it is important to use as much visual material as possible, to help them empathise with children's experiences at that time.

The chapter also asks children to think about the causes and effects of wars, and to make links between their learning about the Second World War and other examples of war which may be taking place now, and the effects of all wars on children's lives. This topic provides a good opportunity to invite a guest speaker to talk about their wartime experiences to the class and also for children to look at local history, by investigating the impact of the war on their local area.

| | OBJECTIVES | MAIN ACTIVITY |
|---|---|---|
| **Lesson 1** P | To place events, people and changes into correct periods of time. To identify and describe reasons for, and results of, historical events, situations and changes in the periods studied. | Children create a timeline of the 20th century and another for the Second World War. |
| **Lesson 2** | To find out about the past from first-hand sources. To communicate their knowledge in a variety of ways. | Children learn about the Blitz and create dramatic scenes of being bombed. |
| **Lesson 3** | To know about characteristic features of the period studied. To communicate their knowledge in a variety of ways. | Children learn about evacuation. They create name labels to wear as 'evacuees' during role play. |
| **Lesson 4** P | To find out about the past from a variety of sources. To recognise that the past is represented and interpreted in different ways. | Reading fictional and first-hand accounts of evacuation leads children to consider differences between sources. |
| **Lesson 5** | To find out about the past from a variety of sources. To communicate their knowledge in a variety of ways. | Children learn about rationing and work out ration allowances. |
| **Lesson 6** | To find out about the past from a variety of sources. | Learning about the women's land army leads the children to a debate on the subject. |
| **Lesson 7** | To find out about the past from a variety of sources. To communicate their knowledge in a variety of ways. | In groups, children research a topic and create a display of their findings. |
| **Lesson 8** P | To find out the past from a variety of sources. To communicate their knowledge in a variety of ways. | Children consider the impact of air raids and bombing using a first-hand account. |
| **Lesson 9** P | To find out about the past from oral and written accounts. To ask and answer written questions, and read information. | Children learn about first-hand memories of war from a visitor and/or photocopiable sheet. |
| **Lesson 10** | To find out about the past from newspapers. | Investigating newspapers from the Second World War leads children to write their own article. |
| **Lesson 11** P | To communicate their knowledge in a variety of ways. | Children consider refugees during the Second World War and today. |
| **Lesson 12** | To select and organise historical information. | Children draw comparisons between the Second World War and wars and terrorist acts today. |

# When did the Second World War take place?

## Objectives
● To place events, people and changes into correct periods of time.
● To identify and describe reasons for, and results of, historical events, situations and changes in the periods studied.

## Vocabulary
twentieth century, decade, significant

## Resources
A 20th-century timeline showing a few key dates, including the start and finish of the Second World War; large blank timeline for the wall, covering the period of the war; the photocopiable sheet 'The Second World War' on page 59, cut up into cards.

## Links
NLS Y3 T2 Text 17: to make clear notes; Y4 T2 Text 23: to collect information from a variety of sources and present it one simple format.

## Background
Children find time and chronology one of the most difficult concepts to grasp. It is important, therefore, to provide them with as many varied opportunities as possible to develop this understanding. By this stage in children's learning some will be beginning to understand the significance of dates, but they are still likely to need considerable support in using them on a timeline and in ordering events chronologically. For this reason, the assembling of information on the class timeline is suggested as a whole-class activity, where you can observe, prompt and support children in their attempts to sort and sequence dates and information about the Second World War.

## Introduction
● Explain to the children that they are going to begin to answer the question: *What were the key events and who were the significant people during the Second World War?*

## Main teaching activity
● Direct the children's attention to the large outline timeline of the 20th century on the wall. Put a few key dates on it and significant events, such as the world wars, landing on the moon and so on.
● Briefly tell the story of the Second World War using page 59.
● Put up, below the 20th-century timeline, an expanded blank timeline just to cover the war years - this will provide the children with enough space to add information and pictures.
● Give out a set of cards from the photocopiable sheet on page 59 to the children and ask them to find the right places for their cards on the timeline of the Second World War.
● They can continue to develop the information on both the timelines throughout the topic, distinguishing between wartime events and events that took place at other times in the 20th century.

## Plenary
● Devise a set of questions and ask about the information on the timeline, for example: *How many years did the Second World War last? What was the first significant event in the War? Who do you think were the most important people in the War?*
● Give suggestions for research, such as finding photographs of significant people.

## Differentiation
Direct appropriate questions to children of different abilities during the introduction and plenary. Ensure cards containing simpler information are given to less able readers in the timeline activity.

# The Blitz

## Objectives
● To find out about the events, people and changes from first-hand sources.
● To communicate their knowledge and understanding of history in a variety of ways.

## Vocabulary
bombing, Blitz, explosion, damage

## Resources
Video clips and photographs showing bomb damage, such as www.historyplace.com/ worldwar2/timeline/ london-blitz.htm and images in the CD-ROM for History 5 in the *Ready Resources* series (Scholastic).

## Links
NLS Y3 T2 Text 17: to make clear notes; Y4 T2 Text 23: to collect information from a variety of sources and present it in one simple format.
NLS Y3-4 Sentence level work: sentence construction and punctuation using speech marks and other dialogue punctuation in writing.
NC PSHE & citizenship KS2: (2a) to research, discuss and debate topical issues, problems and events.

## Background
Although children see a great deal about war in the form of pictures, newspaper reports and television reportage today, they may still find it very difficult to empathise with children experiencing terrible events such as the bombing of their home, town or city. The activity in this chapter aims to allow children opportunities to discuss their understanding with the teacher, with their peers and then to set it down in direct speech. They may also have the opportunity to re-enact what they have understood about bombing at the end of the lesson. This range of experiences will help them to come to terms with and develop some real knowledge and understanding of a very difficult part of history.

## Introduction
● Talk to the children and ask them what they know about what happens during wartime. They may know about bombing from their experience of watching television news reports.
● Explain that a great deal of bombing happened both in Britain and Germany, as well as other parts of Europe and the world, during the Second World War.
● Tell the children that the German bombing of Britain is known as the 'Blitz'.
● Say that in this lesson they will begin to try to understand what it was like during the bombing, which was especially bad in large cities such as London, Coventry, Birmingham, Manchester and Glasgow.

## Main teaching activity
● Show video clips or pictures of the bombing and its aftermath.
● Discuss what it must have been like for people and children living there.
● Explain how much of the bombing happened at night. How easy do they think it would be to sleep at night? What must it have sounded and smelt like? What must it have felt like to not only lose your house but also the whole street in which you lived? Put key words on the board.
● Organise the class into pairs or small groups to write a short dramatic scene about being in a house when the bombing started. Explain that the children are writing a script to act out, so that they should use direct speech.

## Plenary
● Provide time for the children to rehearse and for some pairs or small groups to perform their scenes for the rest of the class.

## Differentiation
Mixed ability pairs or groups will provide support for less able children.

# Evacuees

### Objectives
● To know about characteristic features of the period studied.
● To communicate their knowledge and understanding of history in a variety of ways.

### Vocabulary
evacuee, evacuate, evacuation

### Resources
Pictures of evacuees and internet resources, such as www.bbc.co.uk/dna/ww2/c1162; cards punched with two holes and string for children to thread through them to hang around their necks.

### Links
NC English KS2: En1 (3) to talk effectively as members of a group.
NC English KS2: En1 (4a) to create, adapt and sustain different roles, individually and in groups.

## Background
Heavy bombing by the Germans of towns and cities where munitions were being produced, or where ships, aircraft and other essential items were being manufactured, meant that these areas were considered no longer safe for children to live in. Children considered old enough to be removed from their parents were therefore re-housed in areas less likely to be bombed. This activity is mainly focused on enabling children to appreciate the reasons for and the trauma associated with evacuation.

## Introduction
● Discuss with the children the meaning of the words, *evacuate*, *evacuation* and *evacuee*. Make sure they understand both the general and specialised meanings.

## Main teaching activity
● Look at pictures of evacuees in books and from the internet. Encourage the children to note what clues in the pictures tell us that these children are evacuees, for example, their small suitcases, bags and name cards.
● Explain some of the background about the children, such as the fact that, for many, it was the first time they would have left their home town or city and probably the first time that they would have been away from their parents.
● Ask the class to think about how these children might have felt, and discuss whether they would necessarily all have felt the same. For example, some might have been excited by the adventure. (Make sure you take particular care if there are any children in the class from an orphaned, fostered or refugee background.)
● Give the children each a card and a piece of string to make a name label and ask them to wear it.
● Organise the children into pairs and ask them to create a role play.

## Plenary
● Ask pairs of children to perform their role play. The children can then discuss, still in role, what has happened to them and how they are feeling in their new homes.

### Possible role-play scenarios
● Two children arrive at a farm. Neither has ever been to a farm before. They are very excited and interested.
● A brother and sister arrive at a house where they are met by a grumpy old man.
● Two children meet at a tumbled-down old house with a big happy family in it, with children of their own ages.

## Differentiation
Organise the class to work in mixed ability pairs to provide support for the less able children.

# Sources on evacuees

## Background
The immediacy and authenticity of first-hand accounts, retelling the experiences of evacuees, are perhaps in many ways the best sources for young children to use. Despite problems with the level and style of language, which is, of course, not necessarily written for children, the vivid quality and detail in these real accounts will give children an experience that is as close to the event itself as is possible. There is also an excellent opportunity to make real links with the teaching of literacy, through introducing children to different styles of writing, aimed at different audiences.

## Introduction
● Explain to the class that they are going to read and hear an account written by a person who was actually evacuated from her home as a child.
● Tell them that they are going to find out what sources tell us about the experiences of evacuees.

## Main teaching activity
● Read to the class some stories written about the experiences of evacuees, including fiction and first-hand accounts.
● Discuss the different sorts of information each source contains, for example: in first-hand accounts, there is more factual detail; the fiction contains a great deal of description of children's emotions and feelings.
● Give out copies of the photocopiable sheet 'My life as an evacuee' on page 60 and read through the account with the class. Make sure the children understand any unfamiliar words and expressions.
● Give the children a writing frame to complete with the headings: *Stories tell us* and *Accounts of remembered experiences*.
● Work with the children to complete the first few key points from the stories they have heard.
● Organise the children to work in pairs to re-read the account on the photocopiable sheet and to note down the key points from this on their writing frame.

## Plenary
● During the plenary, ask the children to explain why they think the versions are told differently.
● Ask the children to consider whether they preferred reading the story or the first-hand account and what they have learned about evacuation from each version.

## Differentiation
Prepare the writing frame to match the needs of the different abilities in your class.

# Experiences of rationing

## Objectives
● To find out about the events, people and changes studied from an appropriate range of sources of information.
● To communicate their knowledge and understanding of history in a variety of ways.

## Vocabulary
rations, rationing

## Resources
Example of a real wartime ration book, or a photograph of one from a book or website, such as http://www.circlecity.co.uk/wartime/misc/ration.php; written resources, for example, from www.bbc.co.uk/dna/ww2/A2756298

## Background
Merchant ships bringing food supplies to Britain were under attack from enemy ships and aeroplanes during the war. It was part of enemy strategy to try to weaken Britain by causing hardship to the population. At the same time, the number of men available to work on farms and in the food industry was seriously depleted, since they had been sent away to fight. Consequently, there were widespread shortages of all types of food – some of which could not be provided at all. The government decided to regulate the amount of food allowed to each person on a daily basis, as they would for soldiers. This was known as 'rationing'. Ration books were issued to every household, showing exactly what was allowed. In January 1940, the first rationing began and changes were made as food shortages became worse during the war.

An adult's ration allowance

| | |
|---|---|
| Butter 50g (2oz) | Tea 50g/2oz |
| Bacon/ham 100g/4oz | Jam 450g/1lb every 2 months |
| Margarine 100g/4oz | Sweets 350g/12oz every 4 weeks |
| Sugar 225g/8oz | Meat to the value of 1s. 2d. per week |
| Milk 3 pints (later 2 pints) | (about 5-6p today) |
| Cheese 50g/2oz | Eggs – one a week. |

## Introduction
● Show the class an example of a wartime ration book, or alternatively a picture of one. Ask if they know what it was for.

## Main teaching activity
● Discuss the meaning of rationing and rations. Talk about how this is the way food is allocated in the army - soldiers and sailors are given their 'rations'. In wartime, everyone was treated like this.
● Give the children the list of daily rations (above) and explain that this is what one person would be allowed a day. Also give out a list of simple imperial weights and measures.
● Divide the class into four or five groups according to mathematical ability. Set each group a task according to their ability, for example, to work out the ration allowance for one person for two days, and so on.
● Go through one or two examples with the whole class to show them how to work with the imperial measures.

## Links
NC Mathematics KS2: Ma2 (1a) to make connections in mathematics and appreciate the need to use numerical skills and other knowledge when solving problems in other parts of the curriculum.

## Plenary
● Allow time for the children to make a list of the rations they would like to have for one day and share these with the class.

## Differentiation
Support will be needed for children of weaker mathematical ability and for those who have difficulty working with different measures.

# The women's land army

### Objectives
● To find out about the events, people and changes studied from an appropriate range of sources of information.

### Vocabulary
rations, rationing, shortage

### Resources
Pictures, books, packs and other sources of information about the women's land army; photographs and illustrations of modern-day women; useful websites include www.spartacus. schoolnet.co.uk/2WWland army.htm and http://www. learningcurve.gov.uk/ homefront/women/land/

### Background
Alongside rationing, as an attempt to combat food shortages, the government employed another strategy, which was to encourage women to leave their work in the home and to work on the land to produce food crops. These women were known as 'the women's land army'. Women, especially married women, were not expected on the whole, to go out of the home to work prior to the war. They were seen as homemakers and mothers. Indeed, many professional women, such as teachers, were made to give up their paid employment once they married! This idea of encouraging women to work in factories and as ambulance drivers, as well as on the land, was therefore seen primarily as an emergency measure, only needed during wartime while the men were away.

### Introduction
● Ask the children if they have heard of the women's land army.
● Suggest that they try to work out what it was and provide an explanation if necessary.

### Main teaching activity
● Ask the children if their mothers go out to work and what sort of jobs they do. (Treat this issue sensitively, explaining that neither way of life is better than the other.)
● Explain how, before the Second World War, mothers like theirs would not be expected to work outside the home, but that, when the war began, most of the men of working age were sent away to fight. This meant that the women had to help to grow food on the farms.
● Spend some time talking about why women stayed at home and what the advantages might be.
● Show the class pictures and photographs of the women's land army. Compare these to pictures of modern-day women.
● Invite the children to point out differences they notice between women in the land army and women in modern times.
● Divide the class into two and set up a short debate about whether it was right for women to go out to work in the war. Give one half the role of those who agree and the other half the role of disagreeing. Explain that they need to think of reasons for and against the idea.

### Plenary
● Conclude by holding a vote on the issue.

### Differentiation
Direct appropriate questions to children of different abilities.

### Links
NC English KS2: En1 (3) to talk effectively as members of a group. NC English KS2: En1 (4a) to create, adapt and sustain different roles, individually and in groups.

# Everyday life in the War

## Objectives
● To find out about the events, people and changes studied from an appropriate range of sources of information.
● To communicate their knowledge and understanding of history in a variety of ways.

## Vocabulary
everyday, queue, utility

## Resources
Pictures and first-hand accounts (such as from www.open2.net/ peopleswar/children.html); direct oral accounts (either from a visitor or using, for example, http:// timewitnesses.org/ evacuees/index.html); recordings of wartime songs (for example, from www.jilldaniels.com/ WARTIME.htm); computers or large sheets of paper and art materials.

## Links
NLS Y3 T2 Text 17: to make clear notes; Y4 T2 Text 23: to collect information from a variety of sources and present it in one simple format. NC ICT KS2: (1a) to talk about what information they need and how they can find and use it. NC Art and design KS2: (1a) to select and record from first-hand observation. NC Music KS2: (4d) to learn how time and place can influence the way music is created, performed and heard.

## Background
During the Second World War food supplies were limited; clothes, furniture, children's toys and a whole variety of goods were sometimes not available at all, or people had to make do with wartime versions, known as 'utility' goods. Clothes were designed to use as little fabric as possible and furniture was made from cheap materials, so that raw materials and money could go into the 'war effort'.

At night it was important that it was as dark as possible so that German bombers were unable to pick out any landmarks or targets. Homes were 'blacked out', with heavy curtains and fines were imposed by air-raid wardens or policemen on people who allowed any light to escape through the curtains.

In urban areas, nightly bombing raids disrupted sleep. People soon became exhausted and began to stay in their homes and sleep under the table rather than go to the Anderson shelters in the bad weather! Many men were asked to 'fire-watch' all night. They then had to go to work the next morning.

People tried very hard to remain cheerful during these dreadful times, and the songs they sang give us a good idea of their courage. Some soldiers' songs from the First World War were used again in the Second World War.

## Introduction
● Prompt the children to think about the question: *What can we find out about life for ordinary people in the war?*
● Discuss what they already know, or can imagine.

## Main teaching activity
● Provide the children with pictures, first-hand accounts and, if possible, ask in a visitor to speak about what they remember about daily life during the Second World War. Use video clips, if available.
● Divide the class into five or six groups and give each group a theme, such as: rationing, shortages and queuing at the shops, air raids and air-raid shelters, fire-watching and the blackout.
● Allow time for working in groups to research their topic area.
● Use computers or give the groups large sheets of paper to make posters showing what they have found out about their topic.

## Plenary
● Display the children's work as part of a class display about the Second World War.

## Differentiation
Provide additional adult support for children with reading and writing difficulties during the research and poster-making activities. More able children could write more about what they have learned.

# Schooldays in the Second World War

## Objectives
● To find out about the events, people and changes studied from an appropriate range of sources of information.
● To communicate their knowledge and understanding of history in a variety of ways.

## Vocabulary
air-raid siren

## Resources
The photocopiable sheet 'An air raid in school' on page 61, one per child; other accounts of air raids (for example, from www.gatesheadgrid.org/westallswar/).

## Background
Air raids were a continued threat in towns and cities during the Second World War and precautions were put in place to try to keep people safe. Sirens were used to signal the beginning and end of air raids. A wailing sound meant that enemy aircraft had been sighted. A single note indicated the 'All Clear', that the air raid was over. However, it was impossible to be sure if the bombers would strike a particular place, so not all air-raid sirens meant raids took place and sometimes there were unexpected attacks.

## Introduction
● Explain that some of the people most seriously affected by war are children and discuss why this might be, for example: they find it frightening; they do not understand what is happening; because they are very young, it has a lasting effect on them.
● Say that they are going to find out about life for children in the war.

## Main teaching activity
● Read to the class the photocopiable sheet 'An air raid in school' on page 61. Discuss with the children how they would have felt and what probably happened when the air-raid siren was heard.
● Give out copies of the account to each child and organise the class into groups of five or six to discuss and answer the following:

1. What does the writer mean by 'the siren sounded'?
2. Why did the children not hurry when they were sent home?
3. How did the children know it was a German bomber?
4. Why does the writer say they 'soon' ran to the safety of their homes?
5. How do you think the children felt when they realised what was happening?
6. Why do you think the writer does not explain these feelings?
7. What is an 'allotment'?
8. Why were the sheds scattered around and the glass shattered?
9. Why do you think the writer tells us about the cabbages, potatoes and onions?
10. People often joked and laughed about what happened in the war. Why do you think this was? How many reasons can you think of?

## Plenary
● Discuss ideas about how it might have felt to be in such a situation.

## Differentiation
Mixed ability groups will provide support for the less able children. Encourage more able writers to answer the questions more fully.

## Links
NLS Y4 T2 Text 17: to scan texts in print or on screen to locate key words or phrases and use these as a tool for summarising text. NC English KS2: En1 (3) to talk effectively as members of a group.

# Life for children in the war

## Objectives
● To find out about the events, people and changes studied from oral and written accounts.
● To ask and answer questions, and to select and record information relevant to the focus of the enquiry.

## Vocabulary
frightened, cities, countryside, abroad

## Resources
Visitor to talk about their childhood memories of the war, or the photocopiable sheet 'My life in the war' on page 62, one per child.

## Links
NLS Y3 T2 Text 17: to make clear notes; Y4 T2 Text 23: to collect information from a variety of sources and present it in one simple format.

## Background
Personal accounts are a very valuable source of information for children. If they are accounts of people's childhood memories, children will be able to empathise well with the experience they hear or read. They will be able to make comparisons and connections with their own lives and understand the difficulties and hardships that children in the war experienced. The best source is a person who can come into the classroom and talk directly to the children, answering their questions about what life was like. Take time beforehand to brief the visitor on the sort of areas you would like them to cover. If a visitor is not feasible, or as an additional activity, an account based on real-life experiences is included on the photocopiable sheet on page 62.

## Introduction
● Explain to the class that they are going to try to find out about the past from accounts of what people remember.
● With the children, compile a list of questions on the board to ask the visitor or to find out the answers to from the written account.

## Main teaching activity
● Introduce the visitor to the class. After the visitor has given a short talk on their memories of the Second World War, let the children ask questions, using the list prepared earlier.
● Make sure the children thank their visitor for spending time with them.
● If you are using the written account, read the photocopiable sheet with the children and ask the children to try to find out the answers to their questions.
● Help the children to create a 'question and answer' chart, with headings for two columns such as: *What we asked* and *What we learned*.
● Support the children as they write down the questions and the answers they can remember from the talk or from reading the written account.
● Suggest that they answer as many questions as they can, but tell them that they may not be able to answer them all.

## Plenary
● Ask the class what answers they put down and allow time for children to complete their charts if they were unable to find all the answers on their own.

## Differentiation
Provide additional adult support for the less able children as they write down the questions and their answers. More able children will be able to ask and answer more difficult questions.

# Local experiences of war

## Objectives
● To find out about the events, people and changes studied from newspapers.

## Vocabulary
newspapers, local, locality

## Resources
Copies of wartime articles from local and national newspapers; information books; large sheets of paper, drawing materials, pens and pencils.

## Background
Newspapers are one of the best sources for giving children a clear understanding of what things were like in the past. They are an easily understood source, familiar to children, and they will be able to relate to the articles they see.

Local libraries are an excellent source for both local and national newspapers. Some libraries have very good local collections and will be able to help you find and make copies of any material that you need. The best articles to search for are those which include illustrations of places in the locality which are still there today. These will engage the children's interest quickly and help them relate to a time in the past that is a very long time ago for them.

## Introduction
● Explain to the children that everywhere in the United Kingdom was affected by the war, and that their own local area would also have been affected.
● Tell the class that in this lesson they are going to see what can be found out from newspapers about what happened in their own area in the war.

## Main teaching activity
● Provide the children with a selection of photographs and short articles from local newspapers during the war. If this proves difficult, use examples taken from the national press.
● Read and discuss the articles with the class and encourage the children to look closely at the pictures.
● Ask the children if they recognise anything in the pictures. Hopefully, they will begin to recognise places in their own local area, and begin to understand what it was like in the area during the war.
● Using a collection of books and other materials, ask the children to write their own newspaper article based on an event they have found out about. Invite the children to illustrate their article using the drawing materials provided.

## Plenary
● Invite individuals to read their finished article to the other children.
● Make a display of all the children's work.
● Encourage a discussion as to what can be learned from newspapers from the past and today.

## Links
NLS Y3 T2 Text 17: to make clear notes.
NC Art and design KS2: (1a) to record from experience and imagination, to select and record from first-hand observation and to explore ideas for different purposes.

## Differentiation
Provide additional adult support for those children with reading and writing difficulties. More able children will be able to research an event in small groups and produce a front cover for a newspaper. Create a writing framework for the newspaper article for the less able.

# Refugees then and now

## Objectives
● To communicate their knowledge and understanding of history in a variety of ways.

## Vocabulary
refuge, refugee, persecution

## Resources
Extract from a fictional account of what it's like to be a refugee, for example: *The Silver Sword* by Ian Serraillier (Red Fox); the photocopiable sheet 'Things I would take with me if I were a refugee' on page 63, one per child; drawing materials.

## Links
NC Art and design KS2: (1a) to record from experience and imagination, to select and record from first-hand observation and to explore ideas for different purposes.
NC English KS2: En1 (3) to talk effectively as members of a group.

## Background
Large numbers of refugees fled across different parts of Europe during the Second World War as enemy troops advanced. This lesson leads children to consider the sort of things that might happen to a refugee in wartime. One of the main concerns for a refugee might be to keep their belongings, and this can become increasingly difficult. This subject will need to be handled sensitively if there are children in the class who are asylum seekers or refugees.

## Introduction
● Explain to the children that they are going to be looking at the following two questions: *What was it like to be a refugee? What is it like to be a refugee today?*

## Main teaching activity
● Talk about what it means to be a refugee.
● Read an extract of a story to the children. Discuss the scenes showing refugees that we see on television today.
● Explain that in the Second World War, many people left their homes and were refugees. This was often because their homes were destroyed by fighting, because they were afraid, or because they were in danger of being captured by enemy troops.
● Ask the children what they think their families would want or need to take with them if they had to leave their home quickly.
● Give each of the children a copy of the photocopiable sheet 'Things I would take with me if I were a refugee' on page 63. Ask the children to draw what they want to take in the caravan. They might be able to take quite a few things.
● Create a short game: announce that, at the first checkpoint on the road, the family is told they cannot use their caravan because it is needed by the army. They have to take only what they can carry. At this point, ask them to cross out the things they have had to leave behind. Further along the road, they are attacked by enemy gunfire and have to run for the trees. Again, they have to leave behind many things. Ask them to cross out what they could not carry while running away from enemy fire. Finally, to escape the country, they have to get a boat. When they arrive, they are only permitted to take on board one small bag. Ask the children to draw a small bag and the things they would try to keep inside it.

## Plenary
● Discuss the difficulties faced by refugees in the Second World War and today.

## Differentiation
Provide support for the less able as required during the refugee game.

# The Second World War and wars today

## Objectives
● To select and organise historical information relevant to the focus of the enquiry.

## Vocabulary
terrorist, terrorism

## Resources
Video clips from news reports; newspaper cuttings; art materials and paper.

## Background
Present-day children are surrounded by images of war and terrorism. They are exposed to news coverage of all different kinds. While this can be alarming for some children, it is, at the same time, a good resource for them to use in comparing wars in the past with the present. They can begin to see that there are close links between what has happened in the past and things that are happening today. This will help children to appreciate and understand the changes made and hardships endured by the civilian population during the Second World War.

## Introduction
● Ask the children to think about what has been in the news recently.
● Discuss what they can remember, or have heard about, for example: terrorists; London bombings; 9/11; the war in Iraq. (Remember to be sensitive to issues that may affect individuals in your class.)
● Prompt them to think about the question: *How do modern wars compare with the Second World War?*

## Main teaching activity
● Talk about wars that the children have heard about.
● Challenge them to remember any wars they have heard about in history, for example: wars between France and England.
● Ask if they have ever seen anything about wars on the television and in the newspapers at home.
● Ask if anyone has heard of what happened in New York on 9/11. Show and discuss video clips and newspaper cuttings about current wars or terrorist attacks. (Take care to be sensitive, as some children in your class may be affected – for example, they may have a family member in the army.)
● Compare the sort of things that happened during the Second World War and wars today.
● Discuss how the wars affect the people who live in the countries involved. Talk about the effects the fighting must have on their lives. Discuss what changes these people have to make.

## Links
NC Art and design KS2: (1a) to record from experience and imagination, to select and record from first-hand observation and to explore ideas for different purposes.
NC English KS2: En1 (3) to talk effectively as members of a group.
NC PSHE & citizenship KS2: (2a) to discuss and debate topical issues, problems and events; (2k) to explore how the media presents information.

## Plenary
● Ask the children to draw their own pictures of wars then and now.
● Encourage children to write short pieces of writing, imagining what it must be like to be in a war situation – either in the Second World War or in the present.

## Differentiation
Direct appropriate questions to children of different abilities.

# The Second World War

| | |
|---|---|
| The Second World War started on Sunday 3 September 1939 and victory in Europe was celebrated on Tuesday 8 May 1945. There was fighting in most of Europe and also in many other parts of the world. Much fighting took place in North Africa and the Far East. | Britain and France declared war on Germany after their leader, Adolf Hitler, had invaded Poland on 1 September 1939. On 10 May 1940 Winston Churchill became the British Prime Minister and led Britain's war effort. |
| The German army invaded France in May 1940 and entered its capital city, Paris, on 14 June. | Between 10 July and 31 October 1940 the Battle of Britain took place. This was when the Royal Air Force Spitfire aeroplanes fought the German Luftwaffe in the skies over southern Britain. |
| Then the Luftwaffe changed their strategy and began to bomb London and other cities. This was a period known as the Blitz. | Hitler decided to invade Russia on 22 June 1941 and Britain and Russia agreed to help each other defeat Hitler. |
| The Americans entered the war on 7 December 1941 after Japan attacked Pearl Harbor in Hawaii. | Italy was an ally of the Germans. Their leader was Benito Mussolini. The Italians surrendered to the American army, however, on 8 September 1943. |
| 6 June 1944 was D-Day. This was when a combined British, American and Canadian force landed on the coast of France to lead a counter-attack against the German army. When news of this was announced, everyone thought that the war would soon be over. Paris was liberated on 24 August 1944 and the German forces surrendered on 25 August. Allied troops then entered Nazi Germany on 11 September 1944. When Russian troops reached Berlin, Adolf Hitler is thought to have killed himself on 30 April 1945. | Finally, Churchill announced the end of the war in Europe on 8 May 1945. VJ day was celebrated on 15 August 1945 after the Americans had dropped two atomic bombs on Japan on 6 August and 9 August 1945. |

# My life as an evacuee

**Joan's story**

My mother took my brother and myself to a big station called Paddington in London. She did not tell us that she would not be coming with us on the train, only that I must hold my brother's hand all through the journey. The whole of my school were there plus the teachers who took care of us. When the train left the platform and my mother still stood standing there, I felt very frightened.

We carried a gas mask over one shoulder and another [bag] containing enough food for the journey over the other. A label pinned on our lapel had our name and school in London. The journey was very long, ten hours in near darkness. On arrival at Penzance Station, we were told to climb onto a lorry and taken to the village hall which was very bright after our dark train journey.

The hall was filled with local people and us children. Ten children were told to stand on the stage whilst the local people chose the children they wanted. My brother and I were the last up onto the stage so at this point only one couple was left. They agreed to take my brother but not me, but I refused to let go of his hand. They reluctantly took us both.

My brother and I were the last to be chosen. Can you imagine what it was like for us? standing there while complete strangers decided if they liked the look of us enough to offer us a home? I think I know how slaves must have felt on the auction block – and we were just six and four years old and a long way from our mother. The last couple didn't want me – just my brother – but I wouldn't let go of his hand, so they had to take us both.

They were Mr and Mrs Opie and they lived on a farm outside Penzance and had five children, two boys and three girls. The elder two boys shortly afterwards were drafted into the army. They were a very kind, warmhearted couple and did their best to comfort us by showing us the cows, sheep, chickens and various farm animals. They also showed me how they made butter and cheese. It was a strange world to move into. I had never seen so much green space before and found it somewhat overpowering.

*(extract taken from http://timewitnesses.org/evacuees/~joan.html)*

# An air raid in school

It is now a whole year since the beginning of the war. This is how one man who was a child at school in Liverpool at the time remembers a sudden attack. In writing his account he talks about the 'Five Minute' rule. This meant that boys who lived no more than five minutes walk from school were to go home as quickly as possible as soon as the air-raid warning was sounded. Boys who lived further away went to shelter in the homes of friends nearby.

On Monday 2 September, whilst we were at school, the siren sounded, and obeying the 'Five Minute' rule, we set off for home. We didn't hurry, but played marbles in Stonefield Road with four other boys. When we turned into Shellingford Road, we heard the sound of an aeroplane flying low over the houses. Looking up, we saw it was a German bomber, then we heard what we thought was the sound of hailstones. It was in fact the sound of machine-gun bullets hitting the road around us! We soon ran to the safety of our homes.

Uncle George had an allotment in Sefton Park. After this raid, he went over to the park to see if there was any damage to the allotment sheds and greenhouses. He found that many of the sheds were scattered all over the area and the greenhouses had all the glass panels shattered. He also found that most of his cabbages, potatoes and onions were high up in the trees, having been blown there by the explosions.

An extract from *Children of the Blitz* by Ken Blasbery

# My life in the war

When we first heard the news that the war had begun, we were very frightened. Many people went to church that night to pray that it would not be too bad. Sadly, our way of life did change during the war and things were often very bad for grown-ups and children.

There was less and less food as the years went by. The government decided to ration everyone's food in 1940, so that there would be enough to go round. In 1941 clothes were rationed and, in 1942, even sweets were rationed. I remember how the ice-cream van stopped coming to the end of the road, and how there was no sugar candy. We were always being warned to play carefully and not spoil our clothes. Shoes had to be mended at home because there were no new ones in the shops. There were hardly any toys and we were told to listen to the radio and read the newspapers to find out about the fighting in France and other places. I did not see my father at all during the war.

So much time had to be spent queuing for food to arrive in the shops that our mother had less time for housework. We had to work in our home to help our mother and I had to help by waiting in the queues too. It was very frightening for us at night because there was often bombing. We had to get out of bed and go into the Anderson shelter in the garden. It was very dark because of the blackout. There were many tales of enemy spies in the towns and countryside, which also frightened me.

Many children were sent away and were called 'evacuees'. They were sent away from big towns and cities which were badly hit by bombs. Some of my friends were sent to a nearby town or farm in the country, and some were sent abroad to America or Australia. Most children found it extremely frightening to be sent away from their homes and parents.

In school, lessons were difficult because of the air raids and practices. We had to stop lessons and practise wearing gas masks, which were horrible, and also practise going into the school shelters. As the war went on, there was less and less paper for books and for artwork. Our teacher painted newspaper white for us to draw on. In the winters it was very cold because there was no fuel for heating the schools and we did our lessons wearing our coats.

# Things I would want to take with me if I were a refugee

In the caravan below draw pictures of items that you would take with you if you had to evacuate from your home.

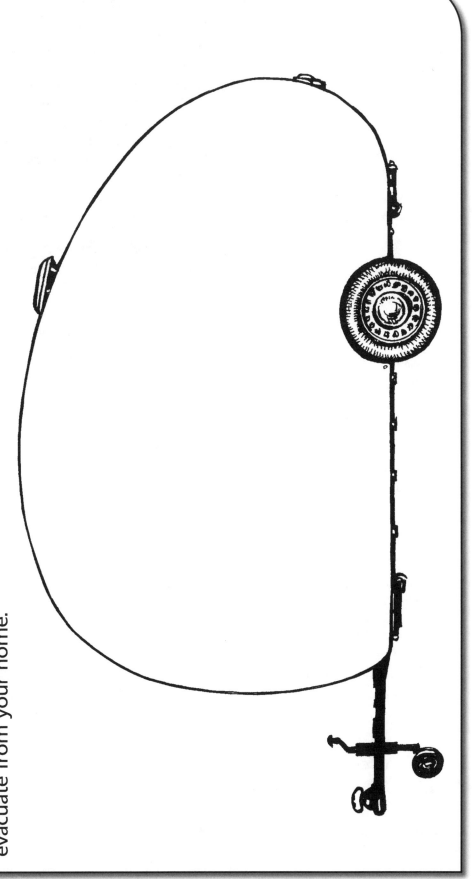

# CHAPTER 4

# Ancient Egypt

This chapter supports teachers in finding and dealing with images of artefacts, ancient sites and excavations from Ancient Egyptian civilisation, and also with the lives and beliefs of people in Ancient Egyptian society. In order to involve the children, links are made with modern-day Egypt, and the area is contextualised in terms of its location, natural features and cultural characteristics. Use is also made of children's own experiences, perhaps in visiting the country, or from television and film, to make links between the present day and the past. A really useful resource is the website of the British Museum at www.ancientegypt.co.uk/menu.html.

Links are also made with other areas of the primary curriculum, in particular with art, ICT, drama, citizenship and geography, as well as consistent links to the national strategies, which occur throughout.

| | OBJECTIVES | MAIN ACTIVITY |
|---|---|---|
| **Lesson 1** (P) | To ask and answer questions, and to select and record information. To know about characteristic features of the period studied. To find out about the past from a variety of sources. | Children find Egypt on a globe and begin to locate places and historic sites within Egypt. |
| **Lesson 2** (P) | To place events, people and changes into correct periods of time. To communicate their knowledge in a variety of ways. | Together, children create a timeline for the Ancient Egyptians. |
| **Lesson 3** | To find out about the past from artefacts. | Making detailed drawings helps children to study artefacts. |
| **Lesson 4** | To find out about the past from historic sites. To ask and answer questions, and to select and record information. To communicate their knowledge in a variety of ways. | Children learn about Rameses II and role play an interview with him. |
| **Lesson 5** | To find out about the past from a variety of sources. To communicate their knowledge in a variety of ways. | Children consider the value of different sources in learning about Ancient Egypt. |
| **Lesson 6** (P) | To know about characteristic features of the period studied. To know about social, cultural, religious and ethnic diversities. | Children study hieroglyphics and invent their own picture writing. |
| **Lesson 7** (P) | To know about characteristic features of the period studied. To know about social, cultural, religious and ethnic diversities. To find out about the past from historic sites. | Children learn about the pyramids and make a paper model. |
| **Lesson 8** | To know about social, cultural, religious and ethnic diversities. To find out about the past from historic sites. | Studying the Valley of the Kings leads the children to write a descriptive poem. |
| **Lesson 9** | To know about social, cultural, religious and ethnic diversities. To find out about the past from artefacts and historic sites. | Children learn about Tutankhamun and complete starter sentences about his tomb. |
| **Lesson 10** | To know about social, cultural, religious and ethnic diversities. To find out about the past from artefacts and historic sites. | In groups, children research mummies and how they were made. |
| **Lesson 11** | To know about social, cultural, religious and ethnic diversities. To find out about the past from written sources. | After looking at the Book of the Dead, children create their own Ancient Egyptian book of spells. |
| **Lesson 12** (P) | To recall, select and organise historical information. To use dates and historical vocabulary. To communicate their knowledge in a variety of ways. | Children review what they have learned and complete a class book. |

# Finding Egypt on a map or globe

## Objectives
● To ask and answer questions, and to select and record information relevant to the focus of the enquiry.
● To know about characteristic features of the period studied.
● To find out about the events, people and changes studied from an appropriate range of sources of information.

## Vocabulary
Egypt, historic site, Nile delta

## Resources
Map or globe of the world; photographs and pictures of Egypt and its historic sites from, for example www.ancientegypt.co.uk/menu.html; the photocopiable sheet 'A map of Ancient Egypt' on page 77, enlarged for display.

## Links
NC Geography KS2: (1a) to ask geographical questions; (2a) to use appropriate geographical vocabulary; (2c) to use atlases and globes, and maps and plans at a range of scales.
NC PSHE & citizenship KS2: (4b) to think about the lives of people living in other places and times, and people with different values and customs.

## Background
Children may have some general knowledge of Egypt from their own visits on holiday and it is worth finding out what they already know. They may also have some knowledge of Ancient Egypt from incidental reading, watching television or films set there. This lesson sets the study in context, both geographically and visually, so that children can locate Egypt on a map and become more familiar with famous landmarks and characteristic geographical and cultural features.

## Introduction
● Prompt the class to begin thinking about Ancient Egypt with questions such as: *Where is Egypt? Who has been there? Who has seen anything about Egypt in films or on the television?*

## Main teaching activity
● Ask the class what they know about the geography of the country – what are the rural areas like and what are the towns like?
● Ask them what images come into their mind when they think of Egypt.
● List the things they say.
● Add the comments of anyone who might have been there to the list.
● Help the children locate Egypt on a map or globe of the world.
● Ask which continent Egypt belongs to.

● Share with the children photographs and pictures of key places and historic sites  - such as Cairo, Alexandria, Giza, Aswan, Luxor, Karnak, Abu Simbel, Valley of the Kings and so on, as well as general photographs of the landscape.

## Plenary
● Display the enlarged copy of the photocopiable sheet 'A map of Ancient Egypt' on page 77 on a wall. Ask for volunteers to place the pictures of the Nile and other major sites on the outline map of Ancient Egypt. (You may find it best to place the pictures around the outside of the map and draw lines to their locations.)

## Differentiation
Provide support as needed and direct appropriate questions to children of differing abilities.

# Timeline activities

## Objectives
- To place events, people and changes into correct periods of time.
- To communicate their knowledge and understanding of history in a variety of ways.

## Vocabulary
Ancient Egypt, BC, ad

## Resources
Large blank timeline, divided into centuries from 3000 years BC to 2000 years AD; pictures and photographs of historic sites and artefacts from Ancient Egypt; the photocopiable sheet 'Information cards' on page 78, cut up into cards.

## Links
NNS Y3–4: number sequences, place value and ordering.
NC Mathematics KS2: Ma2 (2a) to recognise and continue number sequences formed by counting on or back.

## Background
Children find time and chronology one of the most difficult concepts to grasp. In particular the system of dating the years before Christ is very hard to grasp. It is important, therefore, to provide them with as many varied opportunities as possible to develop this understanding. By this stage in children's learning some will be beginning to understand the significance of dates, but they are still likely to need considerable support in using them on a timeline and in ordering events chronologically. For this reason, the assembling of information on the class timeline is suggested as a whole-class activity, where you can observe, prompt and support children in their attempts to sort and sequence a set of information cards about Ancient Egypt.

## Introduction
- Look at pictures and photographs of historic sites and artefacts from Ancient Egypt.
- Ask the children the questions: *When were the Ancient Egyptians around? How long ago did they live?*

## Main teaching activity
- Provide a large blank timeline for the wall, with 'BC' marked at the end.
- Explain the meaning of 'BC' (that is: the years before the birth of Christ). Point out how, as these dates count up to the year of Christ's birth, they are in reverse order (going backwards) and are therefore similar to negative numbers.
- Practise counting backwards with the class, in single digits, then in tens, and finally in hundreds.
- Give out the set of cards from the photocopiable sheet on page 78. Ask individuals to read out the text and then let the children work together to fit them onto the timeline.

## Plenary
- Play a short game, challenging the children to find the right card or date, to test their understanding of the chronology on the timeline.

## Differentiation
Match questioning and the timeline activities to the differing abilities within the class and provide further support for the less able children as needed. Extend the activity for more able children to include a few AD dates to show just how far back in time the Ancient Egyptians existed.

# Finding out about Ancient Egypt from artefacts

## Objectives
● To know about characteristic features of the period studied.
● To find out about the events, people and changes studied from artefacts.

## Vocabulary
artefact, replica

## Resources
Art materials and paper; variety of pictures and replica Egyptian artefacts (artefacts can often be obtained from the local museum service if ordered well in advance and the British Museum Compass website at www.thebritish museum.ac.uk/compass has a good selection of photographs).

## Background
Children can learn a great deal from working with real objects from the past. The objects need to be explained within a meaningful context, however, so that the child is more able to relate to them and see their function. In addition to learning new information and knowledge about the period studied, the use of artefacts as 'clues' about the past can also help develop children's skills in asking historical questions. It can promote their ability to think, to make inferences and deductions, as well as encouraging them to rely on their own interpretations and to be critical of the sources they use. All these skills and qualities will be useful for their future intellectual development.

## Introduction
● Tell the class that they are going to try to answer the following question: *What do objects tell us about Ancient Egypt?*

## Main teaching activity
● Provide the children with a variety of pictures and replica artefacts.
● Discuss with the class what the children think they were probably used for, what they were made from and who might have used them.
● Go on to explain what they actually are and what they tell us about the Ancient Eygptians. The children might also find it interesting to consider where they were found.
● Give out art materials and, making sure all the children have a clear view of one or more of the artefacts, ask the class to make detailed observational drawings of an Ancient Eyptian artefact.

## Plenary
● Together with the class, make a display the children's drawings and information notes. Ask for volunteers to point out their drawing and to describe to the rest of the class what the picture shows and what their artefact would have been used for.

## Differentiation
More able children can write a brief description of their artefact in the form of a museum notice, including comments on what it tells us about life in Ancient Egypt. Less able children may need extra support in the observational drawing activity.

## Links
NLS Y3 T2 Text 17: to make clear notes.
NC Art and design KS2: (1a) to record from experience and imagination, to select and record from first-hand observation and to explore ideas for different purposes.

# Using pictures of statues and historic sites

## Objectives
● To find out about the events, people and changes studied from historic sites.
● To ask and answer questions, and to select and record information relevant to the focus of the enquiry.
● To communicate their knowledge and understanding of history in a variety of ways.

## Vocabulary
pharaoh, temple, statue

## Resources
Collection of pictures and photographs of sites and statues related to Rameses II (a useful website is www.sangha.net/ messengers/Ramses-II .htm); simple timeline of Rameses' life; writing frame for the interview questions and answers; art materials and paper.

## Links
NLS Y4 T2 Sentence 3: sentence construction by understanding the significance of word order. NC English KS2: En1 (3) to talk effectively as members of a group. NC Art and design KS2: (1a) to record from experience and imagination, to select and record from first-hand observation and to explore ideas for different purposes.

## Background
A very useful pharaoh to study in relation to historic monuments is Rameses II. Rameses II was also known as Rameses the Great, partly because he built many monuments, including those at Abu Simbel, the temples at Karnak and Luxor, and many huge statues of himself. Rameses reigned between 1279BC and 1212BC and is one of the most famous of the Egyptian pharaohs. The temples at Abu Simbel were created out of a sandstone cliff. One of the temples has an entrance flanked by four colossal seated statues of Rameses himself (over 20m high). He also built a temple for his favourite wife, Nefertari. Another colossal statue of Rameses II stands before a pylon (gateway) of the great temple of Amun in Karnak, which is famous for being the largest columned room in the world. Numerous examples of these monuments, built to celebrate and enhance his power, can be found on the internet, for example: www.tiscali.co.uk/reference/ encyclopaedia/hutchinson/m0020267.html.

## Introduction
● Introduce this session with the question: *What do statues and important sites tell us about Ancient Egypt?*
● Explain to the class that they are going to study some of the buildings made by one of the most famous pharaohs of all, Rameses II.

## Main teaching activity
● Look at pictures of statues of Rameses II and of the buildings he created. Use a timeline to show when he was pharaoh.
● Discuss the role of the pharaohs in Ancient Egypt. Ask what the children think the pharaohs did. Why they were so important? What were their powers?
● Talk about the huge scale and expense of making these objects and buildings.
● Encourage the children to make inferences about the sort of person Rameses was from their observation of these pictures.
● Organise the class to work in pairs. Encourage the pairs to devise and write some interview questions for Rameses II, using a writing frame to help them, and then to role play the interview, with one child asking the questions and the other providing answers based on what has been learned about Rameses during the lesson.

## Plenary
● Children can complete their work by making drawings of Rameses II.

## Differentiation
Working in mixed ability pairs will provide support for the less able.

# Classifying sources

## Objectives
● To find out about the events, people and changes studied from an appropriate range of sources of information.
● To communicate their knowledge and understanding of history in a variety of ways.

## Vocabulary
source, classify

## Resources
Range of sources, taken from resource packs, books and the internet (useful sites include www.ancient egypt.co.uk; www.bbc.co.uk /history/ancient/egyptians; www.discoveringegypt. com; useful CD-ROM resources include *Ready Resources History 5* (Scholastic)); OHP (optional); cards; writing frame (see activity), one per group.

## Links
NLS Y4 T2 Text 23: to collect information from a variety of sources and present it in one simple format.
NC English KS2: En1 (3) to talk effectively as members of a group.

## Background
This lesson is designed to develop children's skill in beginning to evaluate the sources they are presented with. The sorting and classifying of sources, according to different criteria, will help the children to begin to stand back from their work and think about the use and value of the different kinds of information they have. The plenary session allows children to reflect on the sources and begin to think critically about their relative use in finding out about the past.

## Introduction
● Explain to the children that they are going to begin to think about the sources, materials and information that they are using to find out about Ancient Egypt. They are going to see what different types of information they have.
● Say that in this lesson they will be answering the questions: *How many different ways can we sort out our sources? How many kinds of source do we have?*

## Main teaching activity
● Provide a variety of historical sources about Ancient Egypt for the children to look at on the whiteboard or overhead projector.
● Discuss what the sources show, for example, in the case of artefacts, what they are made from, what they might have been used for, and who would have used them.
● Give the children a set of cards containing features of the sources that they have identified, for example: these sources are artefacts; these are made of pottery; these are metal; these are drawings; these are forms of writing; these are architecture from Ancient Egypt.
● Organise the class to work in small groups to put the sources together into groups.
● Ask the children to think of a describing word or phrase for the groups they have made.
● Give the children a simple outline writing frame and ask them to put in three headings: 'Artefacts and architecture', 'Written sources' and 'Drawings and paintings'.
● Ask the children to classify the sources they have seen under these headings, either by listing them or making small drawings in the appropriate columns.

## Plenary
● Review the ideas and conclusions the children have arrived at. Ask the children whether they think that some sources are more useful than others in telling us about the past. Why do they think this?

## Differentiation
Working in mixed ability groups will provide support for the less able.

# Writing in Ancient Egypt

## Objectives
● To know about characteristic features of the period studied.
● To know about the social, cultural, religious and ethnic diversities of the societies studied, in Britain and the wider world.
● To find out about the events, people and changes studied from an appropriate range of sources of information.

## Vocabulary
hieroglyphics, glyph, writing system, symbol

## Resources
The photocopiable sheet 'Hieroglyphics' on page 79, enlarged for display.

## Links
NC English KS2: En1 (3) to talk effectively as members of a group.
NC PSHE & citizenship KS2: (4b) to think about the lives of people living in other places and times, and people with different values and customs.

## Background
The word 'hieroglyphics', meaning 'sacred carvings', was given to Egyptian script by the Ancient Greeks. Hieroglyphics were used by the Egyptians for about 3500 years, until about AD400. It is also at this time that the record of Ancient Egyptian history ends. Historians were unable to read hieroglyphics until the discovery of the Rosetta Stone. This broken fragment of stone, discovered by French troops in 1799, contained text written in three different scripts – Egyptian hieroglyphics, Egyptian Demotic (developed from hieroglyphics) and ancient Greek. In 1822 Jean-Francois Champollion, a French scholar of ancient languages, managed to use the two other languages to decipher the hieroglyphics and thus provided a key to their further understanding.

## Introduction
● Explain the lesson objectives to the class and tell them that they are going to try to answer the question: *What were hieroglyphics?*
● Ask who has heard of this word before. Can they explain what it is?
● Say how it was a different, early kind of writing system, which developed from the use of pictures, as did many writing systems.

## Main teaching activity
● Show the class a variety of images from an enlarged copy of the photocopiable sheet 'Hieroglyphics'.
● Discuss what the pictures might mean and see if the children can work out any of them from their appearance.
● Explain their meanings, and discuss why the Ancient Egyptians wrote like this. (For example: hieroglyphics had developed from earlier picture writing.)
● Compare this sort of writing with that in other cultures, such as the Aztecs. (See chapter 7).
● Ask the children to work in pairs to create their own invented form of picture writing and to create a short message. Invite them to swap messages with another pair to try to decipher. The children will need to provide a key (for example, something similar to the Rosetta Stone or a format similar to the photocopiable page on page 79) to enable others to understand their message.

## Plenary
● Look at and share the ideas the children have had for their picture writing symbols. Select volunteers to explain their writing systems.
● Talk about which writings systems are easy to understand and discuss how picture writing compares to having an alphabet.

## Differentiation
Working in mixed ability pairs will provide support for the less able.

# Pyramids, gods and beliefs

## Objectives
- To know about characteristic features of the period studied.
- To know about the social, cultural, religious and ethnic diversities of the societies studied, in Britain and the wider world.
- To find out about the events, people and changes studied from historic sites.

## Vocabulary
pyramid, pharaoh, believe, beliefs

## Resources
Videos and pictures of the pyramids at Giza, for example, from websites, such as www.ancient egypt.co.uk/pyramids/ home.html and www.discoveringegypt. com; the photocopiable sheet 'Make a pyramid' on page 80, one per child; art materials, scissors (child use) and glue.

## Links
NC English KS2: En1 (3) to talk effectively as members of a group. NC Mathematics KS2: Ma3 (2b) to visualise and describe 2D and 3D shapes, especially that of pyramids; (2c) to make and draw 2D and 3D shapes. NC PSHE & citizenship KS2: (4b) to think about the lives of people living in other places and times, and people with different values and customs.

## Background
There are about 80 Ancient Egyptian pyramids. The most famous are the three pyramids at Giza. The largest of these is the Pyramid of King Khufu, known as the Great Pyramid and one of the Seven Ancient Wonders of the World. It is made from limestone blocks, which become gradually smaller at the summit. It has been estimated that there are approximately 2.3 million blocks of stone in the pyramid, and that it weighs about seven million tons. No one knows exactly how the pyramids were built, but the rock was cut from nearby quarries. Some theories suggest that the stones were moved on rollers made from logs and then hoisted into place over earth mounds which were then removed. Inside the pyramid a series of narrow passages lead to the burial chamber of King Khufu, who died about 2600BC. Outside the burial chamber is a Grand Gallery and within the chamber is the king's sarcophagus. A vast treasure store of all the king's belongings would have been buried with him. The other two pyramids were built by his son, King Khafra, and by Menkaure, King Khafra's son.

## Introduction
- Say to the children that in this lesson they will be learning why the Ancient Egyptians made pyramids.

## Main teaching activity
- Show the class videos or pictures of the Great Pyramids at Giza. Discuss the scale of the buildings.
- Tell the children that no one knows exactly how they were built and ask the class how they think the stones might have been moved and lifted into place. Talk about current theories on how this was done.
- Discuss why the class think the pyramids were made.
- Talk about how people in different parts of the world have different ideas, customs and beliefs. Say how, in all beliefs, people are buried or cremated carefully according to the custom of that country.
- Look at pictures taken inside the pyramids and discuss what would have been found inside them.
- Give children a copy each of the photocopiable sheet 'Make a pyramid'. Provide scissors, glue and art materials and let the children make their own model. Ask them to draw a plan of what the inside would have been like.

## Plenary
- Add a picture of the site at Giza to the class timeline.

## Differentiation
Children who work quickly can draw small pictures of the site at Giza as an extension activity. Less able children will need adult support in cutting out and assembling their pyramid models.

# The Valley of the Kings

### Objectives
● To know about the social, cultural, religious and ethnic diversities of the societies studied, in Britain and the wider world.
● To find out about the events, people and changes studied from historic sites.

### Vocabulary
tomb, burial site, Tutankhamun

### Resources
Video clips and photographs of the Valley of the Kings (examples of these can be found in resource packs, such as *Ready Resources History 5* (Scholastic), and on websites such as: http://homepages.tcp.co.uk/~nicholson/egypt/kings.html and www.ashmol.ox.ac.uk/gri/carter/b-gallery03/; enlarged using a computer and whiteboard, or on OHP for whole-class viewing.

### Links
NLS Y3 Word level work: vocabulary extension by collecting new words from reading and work in other subjects.
NC English KS2: En1 (3) to talk effectively as members of a group.

## Background
The Valley of the Kings is on the west bank of the Nile. It contains the tombs of many of the later pharaohs, including Tutankhamun. By the early 20th century, over 60 tombs had been discovered and opened, including those of Seti I, Rameses I, II, III, IV and IX. The tombs were decorated with paintings of scenes about the afterlife. The tomb of Tutankhamun was particularly interesting because of all the items it contained, especially since many other tombs had been emptied in earlier centuries by tomb robbers. It is interesting to note that while the Ancient Egyptians used the Nile delta for farming and living in, they made use of their desert areas for burying their dead.

## Introduction
● Explain that the children are going to find out a little more about the beliefs and practices of the Ancient Egyptians, especially what they did when important people died, such as pharaohs or members of their families.
● Tell the class they are going to think about the question: *What would it be like to walk through the Valley of the Kings?*

## Main teaching activity
● Look at video clips and photographs of the Valley of the Kings. Talk about the size of the valley and the height of its sides. What sounds might the children hear in such a place and what might they feel like if they were in it?
● Discuss why this is an important place in Egypt today, just as it was in ancient times. Explain how, for many years, it was the burial site of the pharaohs and that about 60 kings are buried here. (There are also other burial sites in the vicinity for queens, workers and so on.)
● Tell the class that the famous tomb of Tutankhamun was found here.
● Organise the children to work in pairs or small groups and to imagine they are entering the Valley of the Kings. Discuss words that might describe such a place, such as: *eerie, silent, imposing, frightening, ghostly* and *calm.*
● Using the list of words as a starting point, encourage each group to write a poem imagining they are in the Valley of the Kings.

## Plenary
● Share some of poems with the class, while looking at enlarged images of the Valley of the Kings.

## Differentiation
The more able children could go on to write a descriptive paragraph or an epitaph to a pharaoh. Organise the class to work in mixed ability pairs or groups to provide support for the less able children.

# Tutankhamun's tomb

## Objectives
● To know about characteristic features of the period studied.
● To know about the social, cultural, religious and ethnic diversities of the societies studied, in Britain and the wider world.
● To find out about the events, people and changes studied from artefacts and historic sites.

## Vocabulary
coffin, mummy, artefacts, afterlife

## Resources
Pictures of Tutankhamun's tomb and its contents, found in resource packs or on the internet at websites, such as www.topfoto.co.uk/gallery/tutankhamun/

## Background
Tutankhamun, who ruled from about 1334 to 1325BC, is thought to have been murdered at the age of 18 and he was probably, therefore, not a very important pharaoh. However, his tomb is one of the richest ever found. It was discovered by the archaeologist Sir Howard Carter and its contents are considered an important collection, since many items from tombs of other pharaohs were lost to tomb robbers. The antechamber to Tutankhamun's tomb was piled high with hundreds of objects, such as chariots, decorated with gold, glass and precious stones. Carter found that the tomb had been opened twice, hundreds of years earlier, before he discovered it. The tomb had then been re-sealed and, although it had probably been robbed, as most of the tombs had been, very little had been taken. There were also two life-sized painted wooden figures of the king, an animal couch, boxes, chests, stools and chairs, which had been crammed into the room.

## Introduction
● Explain to the class that in this lesson they are going to learn about one of the most famous discoveries made in the Valley of the Kings: the discovery of the tomb of a pharaoh called Tutankhamun.
● Tell the class a little about Tutankhamun, explaining that he seems to have been killed at quite a young age.
● Say that they are going to answer the question: *What can we find out about the life of Tutankhamun from what was found in his tomb?*

## Main teaching activity
● Show the class a selection of photographs of the items found in the tomb.
● Give the children some sentence starters to help them write sentences about why the objects were placed in the tomb, for example: *The Ancient Egyptians put their personal things in the tomb because …* and *Tutankhamun had his chariots in the tomb because …*
● Talk about how the objects buried with Tutankhamun were not objects that all Egyptians would have had. These were things that a king would want to have with him in the afterlife. What objects do they think that ordinary people might have had if they had been buried in a similar tomb?

## Links
NC English KS2: En1 (3) to talk effectively as members of a group.
NC PSHE & citizenship KS2: (4b) to think about the lives of people living in other places and times, and people with different values and customs.

## Plenary
● Conduct a general discussion about what the children have found out about the burial practices of the Ancient Egyptians.

## Differentiation
Less able children will need adult support when completing their sentences. More able children could go on to write their own sentence starters and complete them.

# Why were mummies made?

## Objectives
- To know about characteristic features of the period studied.
- To know about the social, cultural, religious and ethnic diversities of the societies studied, in Britain and the wider world.
- To find out about the events, people and changes studied from artefacts and historic sites.

## Vocabulary
culture, religion, afterlife

## Resources
Information books, pictures or video clips of mummies, for example, using *Ready Resources History 5* (Scholastic), resources from the British Museum or using websites (such as www.bbc.co.uk/history/ancient/egyptians/mummies_01.shtml or www.ancientegypt.co.uk/mummies/explore/main.html); paper, pens and pencils.

## Links
NLS Y3 T2 Text 17: to make clear notes.
NC English KS2: En1 (3) to talk effectively as members of a group.
NC ICT KS2: (1a) to talk about what information they need and how they can find and use it.
NC PSHE & citizenship KS2: (4b) to think about the lives of people living in other places and times, and people with different values and customs.

## Background
Although considerably shrunken, the embalmed body can be seen when the bandages are removed from a well-preserved mummy. The skeleton, teeth and skin are all present and, in some cases, even the hair remains. The inner organs would have been removed by the embalmer, so that the body could be preserved. The brain was removed through the nostrils with a spiked instrument, but the heart was left in the body. The mummification process took many weeks to complete, and often good-luck charms were placed between the layers of bandages as the body was wrapped. Egyptians mummified their dead so that they could preserve the person's body for their difficult journey into the afterlife. The good luck charms were to help them on their journey. If possible, take the children to visit the British Museum or a local museum where mummies can be seen. Alternatively, use information books, video clips and the internet.

## Introduction
- Open the lesson with the questions: *Why did the Ancient Egyptians make mummies? How did they make them?*
- Explain that it is important to understand why people did things differently in different parts of the world. Discuss how this is part of Ancient Egyptian culture and belief, based on their religion.
- Talk about how there are still many different cultures with different beliefs today and that people do different things according to their religious beliefs.

## Main teaching activity
- Look at pictures of mummies. Discuss how and why they were made.
- Explain the Ancient Egyptian belief in the afterlife and how the body needed to be preserved for the journey there.
- Organise the class to work in groups to research different aspects of the process, for example: the reasons for making mummies; how they were prepared; embalming; how they were bandaged; the removal of the organs; the sealing of the mummy in a sarcophagus; the journey to the afterlife.
- Give out sheets of paper for the children to make notes and sketches and then allow them time to write their information text.

## Plenary
- Compare these beliefs about the treatment of the dead with those of other cultures, such as Christianity and Hinduism. Use the notes and sketches made to begin a class book about the Ancient Egyptians.

## Differentiation
Organise the groups so that less able children work together on simpler tasks, researching from shorter written or viusal sources.

# The Book of the Dead

## Objectives
● To know about characteristic features of the period studied.
● To know about the social, cultural, religious and ethnic diversities of the societies studied, in Britain and the wider world.
● To find out about the events, people and changes studied from written sources.

## Vocabulary
magic spells, afterlife, beliefs

## Resources
Pictures of the Book of the Dead and examples of pages from it, taken from resource packs, books or the internet, such as http://egyptianbookofthedead.org and www.egyptarchive.co.uk/html/book_of_the_dead_index.html; paper and art materials; the photocopiable sheet 'Hieroglyphics' on page 79.

## Links
NLS Y3 T2 Text 16: to write instructions; Y4 T3 Text 21: to assemble and sequence points in order. NC English KS2: En1 (3) to talk effectively as members of a group. NC PSHE & citizenship KS2: (4b) to think about the lives of people living in other places and times, and people with different values and customs.

## Background
Many copies of the Book of the Dead were produced en masse in places called Houses of Life, written there by priests and scribes. They were really books of magic spells, which the Ancient Egyptians believed could protect them. The books were made from papyrus and each contained a collection of about 200 magic spells, written to make the journey to the afterlife safer for the spirit of the dead person.

Hieroglyphics were often used in the background of these books. The eventual discovery of how to read hieroglyphics in the nineteenth century meant that much could be learned from sources like this about the beliefs and practices of the Ancient Egyptians.

## Introduction
● Prompt the children to think about the question: *What was the Book of the Dead?*
● Encourage them to speculate about what it was and what it was for.
● Explain that it was a book of spells made to protect the spirit of a dead person on their journey to the afterlife. This journey was believed to be very dangerous, and the Ancient Egyptians believed that magic spells could protect them.
● Say that in this lesson, they are going to find out more about the Book of the Dead, how it was used and what the Ancient Egyptians believed.

## Main teaching activity
● Show pictures of the Book of the Dead to the children. Explain that it was a book of 200 spells made to protect the spirit of a dead person on their journey to the afterlife.
● Discuss the sort of spells that might have been considered helpful by the Ancient Egyptians, for example: protection from demons. Make a list on the board of the children's ideas.
● Give out paper and art materials and ask the children to create a page for an Ancient Egyptian book of spells. Display an enlarged version of the photocopiable sheet 'Hieroglyphics' on page 79 to help the children illustrate their pages.

## Plenary
● Share some of the children's work and make a wall display.

## Differentiation
Less able children will need adult support when completing their spells and books.

# A book about Ancient Egypt

**Objectives**
● To recall, select and organise historical information.
● To use dates and historical vocabulary to describe the period studied.
● To communicate their knowledge and understanding of history in a variety of ways.

**Vocabulary**
summary, summarise, organise, knowledge

**Resources**
Large blank book; paper; art materials; computers; OHP (optional); the photocopiable page 'Things to make for a book on Ancient Egypt' on page 81.

**Links**
NLS Y3 T2 Text 17: to make clear notes.
NC Art and design KS2: (1a) to record from experience and imagination, to select and record from first-hand observation and to explore ideas for different purposes.
NC ICT KS2: (1a) to talk about what information they need and how they can find and use it.

## Background
The making of a book is a pleasurable experience for young children and it also provides an opportunity for others to celebrate their work. The activity gives both purpose and form to their learning and so motivates the children to produce work of a high standard. In addition, asking children to review what they have learned and to complete further activities using their knowledge provides the teacher with a good opportunity to assess both their learning and the skills and understandings they have developed. The photocopiable sheet 'Things to make for a book on Ancient Egypt' on page 81 suggests a range of open-ended activities that will test the children's abilities across a range of historical skills and concepts.

## Introduction
● Explain to the class that they are now going to make a class book about what they have learned about the Ancient Egyptians.

## Main teaching activity
● Prompt the children to recall what they have learned with the question: *What have we found out about Ancient Egypt?*
● Make a chart on the overhead projector or whiteboard for their answers and divide this under headings such as: 'Beliefs', 'Dress', 'Farming', 'Landscape', 'Maps', 'Timelines', 'Buildings', 'Rulers', 'Book of the Dead' and so on.
● Make these the headings for sections or chapters in the class book and also the themes for groups to work on.
● Organise the children into groups and encourage each group to recall their learning and to develop what they know with further research, using books, resource packs and the internet.
● Provide the children with materials and support them in making a large class book, into which they put their best work, descriptions, pictures, maps, timelines and spells.
● Ask the children what order they think the sections in the book should go. Are there some topics that need to go before others?
● In the course of making the book, assessment tasks can be set as activities, using the photocopiable sheet on page 81.

## Plenary
● Make the class book available for other children and visitors to read in a central location in the school.

## Differentiation
Provide the less able children with support in making their entries for the book. More able children should be encouraged to produce longer pieces of writing and to think of their own in depth questions to research.

# A map of Ancient Egypt

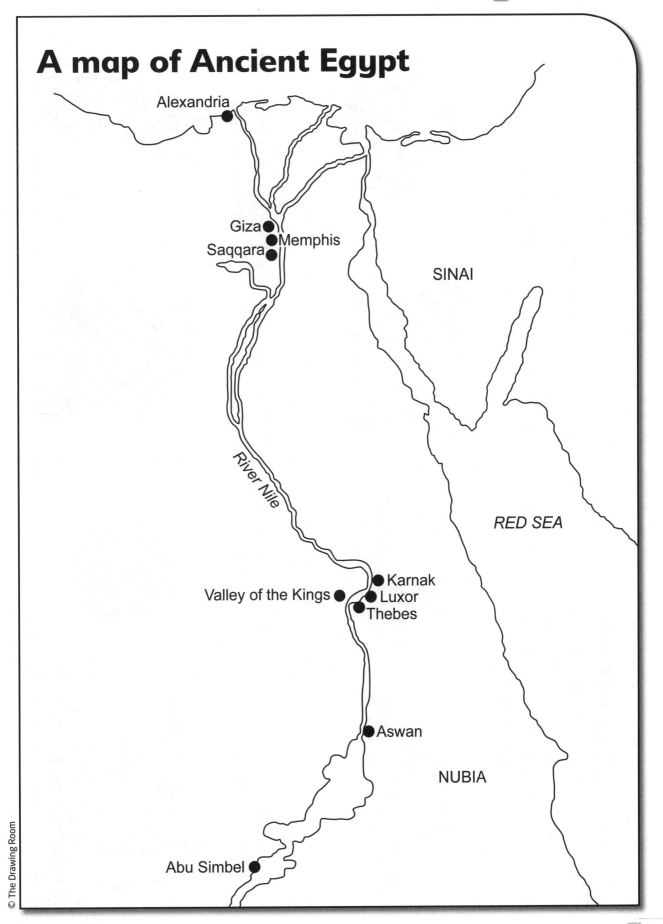

# Information cards

| | | |
|---|---|---|
| 2650BC<br>First pyramid built for Zoser, now at Saqqara | 2500BC<br>Great Pyramid at Giza | 1327BC<br>Tutankhamun's tomb | 1279–1213BC<br>Rameses II and Karnak |
| c1186BC<br>Pylon and statues of Rameses II completed at Luxor | 332BC<br>Alexander the Great conquers Egypt | 196BC<br>The Rosetta Stone was carved | 30BC–AD400<br>Egypt is a province of the Roman Empire |

# Hieroglyphics

| | | | | | |
|---|---|---|---|---|---|
| | vulture | **ah** *(father)* | | reed | **i** *(filled)* |
| | two reeds | **y** *(discovery)* | | arm & hand | **broad a** *(car)* |
| | quail chick | **oo** *(too)* or **w** *(wet)* | | foot | **b** *(boot)* |
| | mat | **p** *(pedestal)* | | horned viper | **f** *(feel)* |
| | owl | **m** *(moon)* | | water | **n** *(noon)* |
| | mouth | **r** *(right)* | | reed shelter | **h** *(hat)* |
| | twisted flax | **h!** *(ha!)* | | placenta | **kh** *(like Scotch 'loch')* |
| | animal's belly | **ch** *(like German 'ich')* | | folded cloth | **s** *(saw)* |
| | door bolt | **s** *(saw)* | | pool | **sh** *(show)* |
| | slope of hill | **k** *(key)* | | basket with handle | **k** *(basket)* |
| | jar stand | **g** *(go)* | | loaf | **t** *(tap)* |
| | tethering rope | **tj** *(church)* | | hand | **d** *(dog)* |
| | snake | **dj** *(adjust)* | You may notice that some hieroglyphs are vowel sounds, these are considered weak consonants and are used when a word begins with a vowel or where it might be confusing without them, like in a name. | | |

# Make a pyramid

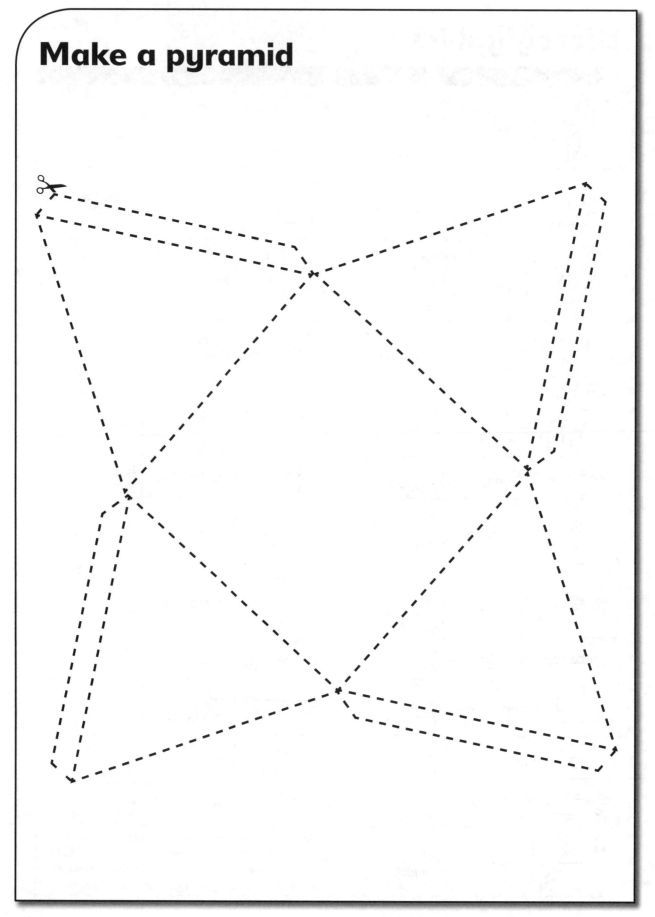

# Things to make for a book on Ancient Egypt

Choose one of these things to make and put into the class book:

1. A timeline of Ancient Egypt
2. A map showing the Nile and the desert
3. A map showing the most important historical sites in Ancient Egypt
4. A picture of a pharaoh
5. A picture of an Egyptian woman and child
6. A description of how papyrus is made
7. A picture of a shaduf
8. A set of pictures showing papyrus being made
9. A map showing the parts of Ancient Egypt which could be farmed with crops
10. A picture of the Book of the Dead
11. An explanation of what the Book of the Dead was used for
12. A photograph of the things found in the tomb of Tutankhamun
13. A written explanation of why these things were in his tomb
14. A photograph of the Valley of the Dead
15. Some notes about what it is like in the Valley of the Dead
16. Pictures of famous pharaohs
17. Pictures of mummies
18. An explanation of why mummies were made
19. Pictures and drawings of objects found in tombs
20. Pictures and photographs of the pyramids at Giza
21. Pictures of Ancient Egyptian statues
22. Pictures of hieroglyphics
23. Puzzles and other writing made using hieroglyphics
24. A picture of the Sphinx.

# CHAPTER 5

# Victorian Britain

The Victorian period is very rich in personalities, scientific discoveries, inventions, and political and social change, all of which brought about eventual advances in the lives of ordinary people. There are major differences between life in the early and late Victorian periods. Changes, such as the requirement for all children to attend school, first introduced in 1870, improvements to public health, vast building programmes and the development of the railways, had an impact on everyone in Britain. Tighter controls on working conditions and the introduction of schooling meant that the lives of many children, at least up to the age of 11 or 12, were considerably altered, compared with their lives at the beginning of Victoria's reign.

| | OBJECTIVES | MAIN ACTIVITY |
|---|---|---|
| **Lesson 1** P | To place events, people and changes into correct periods of time. To ask and answer questions, and to select and record information. To identify and describe reasons for, and results of, historical events, situations and changes in the periods studied. | Children look at a timeline and pictures of children taken over Victoria's reign. |
| **Lesson 2** | To recognise that the past is represented and interpreted in different ways. To find out about the past from portraits and paintings. | Using different paintings, the class comment on how Victorian children are portrayed. |
| **Lesson 3** P | To use dates and vocabulary relating to the passing of time. To find out about the past from census data. | Children look at a census showing the poor and use it to research information. |
| **Lesson 4** P | To use dates and vocabulary relating to the passing of time. To find out about the past from census data. | Children look at a census showing the rich and use it to research information. |
| **Lesson 5** P | To recognise that the past is represented and interpreted in different ways. To find out about the past from written accounts. | Children learn about the work of Lord Shaftesbury and Dr Barnado. |
| **Lesson 6** P | To find out about the past from a variety of sources. To recall, select and organise historical information. To communicate their knowledge in a variety of ways. | A role play of a Victorian lesson enables children to consider education in that period. |
| **Lesson 7** | To use dates and vocabulary relating to the passing of time. To know about characteristic features of the period studied. To identify and describe reasons for, and results of, historical events, situations and changes in the periods studied. | Children compare Victorian and modern-day schooling. |
| **Lesson 8** | To know about characteristic features of the period studied. To know about the social, cultural, religious and ethnic diversity. To find out about the past from visual sources. | Children compare the lives of rich and poor children. |
| **Lesson 9** | To find out about the past from a variety of sources. To recall, select and organise historical information. To communicate their knowledge in a variety of ways. | A study of Victorian leisure time leads children to design a magazine cover for a day out. |
| **Lesson 10** | To know about characteristic features. To find out about the past from a variety of sources. To ask and answer questions, and to select and record information. | Children consider church-going and re-enact a Sunday School lesson. |
| **Lesson 11** P | To ask and answer questions, and to select and record information. To identify and describe reasons for, and results of, historical events, situations and changes in the periods studied. To find out about the past from a variety of sources. | Children debate the issues of improvement in children's lives in the Victorian era. |
| **Lesson 12** | To recall, select and organise historical information. To communicate their knowledge in a variety of ways. | Children take part in a quiz about all they have learned in the topic. |

# Victorian children's lives

## Objectives
- To place events, people and changes into correct periods of time.
- To ask and answer questions, and to select and record information relevant to the focus of the enquiry.
- To identify and describe reasons for, and results of, historical events, situations and changes in the periods studied.

## Vocabulary
early Victorian, late Victorian, period

## Resources
The photocopiable sheet 'Timeline of Victorian Britain' on page 95, one per child and one enlarged for display; pictures, sketches and photographs of children at work, at school, at home and at play, some from the early period and some from late Victorian times.

## Links
NNS Y3-4: number sequences, place value and ordering.
NLS Y5 T1 Text 26: to make notes for different purposes.

## Background
The degree and rate of change, socially, politically and economically, was very rapid between the early and late Victorian periods. At the beginning of Victoria's reign, for example, people would have travelled mainly on foot or on horseback. Yet by the end of the period, there were railways, motorised vehicles and steam-powered sea transport available. This lesson makes this rapid change evident to children, as well as distinguishing between the early and late parts of Victoria's reign, through the use of a timeline of events and developments.

## Introduction
- Begin by asking children what they have already learned about Victorian times.
- Discuss the idea that things were changing very rapidly during the reign of Queen Victoria.
- Explain to the class that they are going to begin to answer the question: *How did children's lives change during the Victorian period?*

## Main teaching activity
- Give out copies of the photocopiable page 'Timeline of Victorian Britain' on page 95 to the children. Explain how things changed greatly over that time.
- Ask the children to try to pick out important events that show what changes took place, for example: the beginning of education for all, the Reform Acts giving men the right to vote, the opening of the Great Western Railway, the numerous inventions and so on. Encourage them to make comments on why these things happened.
- Show the class a series of pictures, sketches and photographs of children at work, at school, at home and at play, some from the early period and some from late Victorian times.
- Ask the children to look at the pictures and think which are from the early Victorian period and which from the later Victorian period.
- Encourage them to use the information on the timeline to guide their decisions, for example: working children in the 1830s, children in Board Schools in the 1890s.
- Ask the children to explain why they have made these decisions.

## Plenary
- Ask volunteers to place the pictures in the right places on a large classroom timeline, which can then become the basis for a wall display. The children can add to the timeline as the topic progresses.

## Differentiation
Match questioning to the differing abilities within the class. The more able can search for additional information and add notes and captions to their timelines. The less able can add illustrations to their timelines.

# Portraits of Victorian children

## Objectives
● To recognise that the past is represented and interpreted in different ways, and to give reasons for this.
● To find out about the events, people and changes studied from portraits and paintings.

## Vocabulary
portrait, painting, interpretation

## Resources
Variety of paintings of Victorian people, each including children (some enlarged for class work), taken from books, resource packs and the internet (for example: www.richard-york.co.uk/past/vicchildren.html); blank cards and pens.

## Background
Portraits are an excellent source of information on people in Victorian times, and also a useful type of stimulus for developing children's historical skills. They provide the opportunity for informed enquiry through the process of asking and answering questions, which are important skills in interrogating sources. The use of portraits is in particular an opportunity to introduce the notion of interpretation to young children. The idea is a difficult one and, by approaching it through the use of visual sources, it will be more accessible to children of this age. They will gradually begin to understand that each portrait we see is the interpretation of the age by that particular artist.

## Introduction
● Before the start of the lesson, arrange a variety of portraits of Victorian people around the room, and have some good examples available in an enlarged format, for whole-class viewing.
● Begin by explaining to the children that they are going to look particularly at the place of children in Victorian times. They are going to think about the question: *How are children represented in portraits and paintings?*

## Main teaching activity
● Using a variety of portraits and paintings of Victorian people and children, ask the children to comment on the way in which the children are portrayed. Where are they positioned? Do they appear important in the pictures? How are they dressed? What are they doing? Do they appear to be happy and playing?
● Encourage the children to make inferences from their observations about the position of children in society at this time and how they think children were treated. Discuss whether this confirms what they have already heard on this subject.
● Provide the children with cards to write captions to describe how they appear, for example: children appear very serious and unhappy in Victorian photographs.

## Plenary
● Provide time for the children to display their written captions alongside the portraits on display.

## Differentiation
Less able children will need adult support when writing their captions. Encourage more able children to write sentences or paragraphs about the pictures and direct them to try to use as much detail as possible from the visual sources to justify their interpretations.

## Links
NLS Y5 T1 Text 26: to make notes for different purposes.
NC English KS2: En1 (3) to talk effectively as members of a group.

# Using the census to investigate the poor

## Objectives
● To use dates and vocabulary relating to the passing of time.
● To know about characteristic features of the period and societies studied.
● To find out about the events, people and changes studied from census data.

## Vocabulary
census, records, poverty

## Resources
Example from an early Victorian local census data of a poor area – available from local libraries or record offices or the photocopiable sheet 'Census extract 1: 1851' on page 96, one per child; computers (optional). Useful websites for census data include www.mape.org.uk/ curriculum/history/ census.htm and www. learningcurve.gov.uk/ FocusOn/census/

## Links
NC English KS2: En1 (3) to talk effectively as members of a group. NC ICT KS2: (1c) to interpret information.

## Background
The census is an excellent source of information. The census began in 1801 and has been completed every ten years since. Early census records, especially before 1851, are unreliable and inaccurate. Information is haphazard and not always logically organised, so that it is difficult to use on a computer system. It is safest, therefore, to use records from 1851 onwards. However, some details from earlier data can be useful in that it gives us an insight into the lives of people at that time.

## Introduction
● Explain the lesson objectives to the class, and ask if anyone has heard of the census before.
● Briefly say what the census is, and how it is done every ten years, so that the most recent one will have been carried out in 2001.
● Tell the class that they are going to look at a Victorian census and to find out information from it.

## Main teaching activity
● Look at local census returns from 1841 and 1851, or use the example provided on the photocopiable sheet 'Census extract 1: 1851' on page 96.
● Explain the meaning of all the headings and discuss a few examples with the class.
● Organise the children to work in pairs to find out information from the data. (It is easier for the children if the information is entered on a computer programme such as Access or Excel.)
● Ask the children to find the answers to some general questions, for example: how many people lived in one house; how many belonged to the family; how many were servants; what sorts of names did they have; what jobs did they do; how many were at school?
● Encourage the children to draw inferences from the answers they get. Do they think the people in this extract were rich or poor? Why?
● Suggest each pair of children pick one child in the census, identify their parents, sisters and brothers, and then write a factual piece containing all the information they find out.

## Plenary
● Ask individuals to share their written pieces. Finally, draw the conclusion that the people in this census extract are probably all quite poor, working class people.

## Differentiation
Mixed ability pairs will provide support for the less able children.

# Using the census to investigate the rich

## Objectives
● To use dates and vocabulary relating to the passing of time.
● To know about characteristic features of the period and societies studied.
● How to find out about events, people and changes studied from census data.

## Vocabulary
census, records, wealth

## Resources
Examples from late Victorian census data – available from local libraries or record offices or the photocopiable sheet 'Census extract 2: 1881' on page 97, one per child; computers (optional). Useful websites on the use of census data include www.mape.org.uk/ curriculum/history/ census.htm and www. learningcurve.gov.uk/ FocusOn/census/

## Links
NC Art and design KS2: (1a) to record from experience and imagination, to select and record from first-hand observation and to explore ideas for different purposes.
NC English KS2: En1 (3) to talk effectively as members of a group.
NC ICT KS2: (1c) to interpret information.

## Background
As well as ordinary people, the census, particularly from the late Victorian period, is an excellent source of information about the lives of the better off, their families and the homes they lived in. By looking at telling details, such as the number of servants in a household, children can quickly see the differences in the lives of the rich and poor.

## Introduction
● Ask if anyone has heard of the census before.
● Briefly explain what the census is, and how it is done every ten years, so that the most recent one will have been carried out in 2001.
● Tell the class that they are going to look at a late Victorian census to try to find out how children from wealthy backgrounds are represented in the census data.

## Main teaching activity
● Look at local census returns from a late Victorian census, obtainable from your local library or record office. If these are difficult to obtain, use the example provided on the photocopiable sheet 'Census extract 2: 1881' on page 97 as an alternative.
● Explain the meaning of all the headings on the census page and discuss a few examples with the whole class to demonstrate how to understand the data.
● Let the children work in pairs to interrogate the data and make searches. (It will be easier for the children to use if it can be entered into a computer programme such as Access or Excel. This will enable them to search and count up items much more quickly.)
● Ask them to find the answers to some general questions for example: who was the head of the household; how did this affect the rest of the family; how many people lived in one house; how many were servants; how many were at school?
● Suggest they pick one family from the census and identify the family members.
● Working in pairs, ask the children to use the information provided by the census to write a short description of the family, with illustrations of how they might have looked.

## Plenary
● Share with the rest of the class some of the notes drawn up from the census data.

## Differentiation
Mixed ability pairs will provide support for the less able children.

# The work of Shaftesbury and Barnardo

## Objectives
● To recognise that the past is represented and interpreted in different ways, and to give reasons for this.
● To find out about the events, people and changes studied from written accounts.

## Vocabulary
philanthropist; significant figure

## Resources
The photocopiable sheet 'Lord Shaftesbury and Dr Barnado' on page 98, one per child; highlighter pens or coloured pencils; pictures and written accounts from books, resource packs and websites, such as www. barnardos.org.uk/who_we_ are/history.htm; www. infed.org/thinkers/ barnardo.htm; www.infed. org/walking/wa-shaft.htm and www.learningcurve. gov.uk/victorianbritain/ industrial/fom1.htm

## Links
NLS Y6 T1 Text 14: writing composition by skills of biographical and autobiographical writing in role.
NC English KS2: En3 (1a) to use form and content to suit a particular purpose.

## Background
Lord Shaftesbury and Dr Barnardo are two key figures in the field of factory reform and child welfare. Although they came from very different backgrounds, both men were affected by the dreadful living and working conditions for the poor, which they saw and read about. Both were extremely determined and would face any opposition to achieve what they knew to be right. They were particularly moved to action by the lives of the poorest children, who lived, worked and died in terrible conditions at that time. Shaftesbury tried to improve working conditions in factories and mines, while Barnardo was concerned about providing decent homes for orphaned and homeless children.

## Introduction
● Talk about what it must have been like for poor children in Victorian times: their homes, work, health, education and so on.
● Ask: *What did people do to improve the lives of poor children?*
● Discuss how some people became concerned about the lives of the very poor children, and how some, such as Shaftesbury and Barnardo, worked hard to help them.

## Main teaching activity
● Give the children each a copy of the photocopiable sheet 'Lord Shaftesbury and Dr Barnado' on page 98 and other written accounts for the children to read.
● Discuss why these two men are remembered as important figures.
● Encourage the children to highlight all the main points in their texts, working through the first point or two with the whole class.
● Ask the children to then use these points to write an account from a different point of view, for example: in the first person, describing their work as if they were either Shaftesbury or Barnado (*My name is… I first became interested in the lives of the poor when…*).
● Ask the children to search on the internet for pictures and further information of their chosen character to assist them in their writing and to illustrate their completed work.

## Plenary
● Ask for volunteers to read their accounts in the role of either Shaftesbury or Barnado.

## Differentiation
Less able children will need adult support when writing their accounts and in adapting to writing in the first person. More able children can search for further information for their first-hand accounts.

# Victorian school life

## Objectives
● To find out about the events, people and changes studied from a variety of sources.
● To recall, select and organise historical information.
● To communicate their knowledge and understanding of history in a variety of ways.

## Vocabulary
Board School, instruction, behaviour, object lesson

## Resources
The photocopiable sheet 'A Victorian lesson' on page 99; extracts from school logbooks; pages from punishment books; inspection reports; internet resources, such as www.bbc.co.uk/schools/ victorians/standard/school/ learning/index.shtml; dressing-up clothes and props.

## Links
NLS Y5 T1 Text 18: writing composition by writing own playscript, applying conventions learned from reading.
NC English KS2: En1 (4a) to create, adapt and sustain different roles, individually and in groups.

## Background
The provision of schooling for all was perhaps one of the most significant changes that took place between the early and late Victorian periods. At the beginning of Victoria's reign, apart from the public schools, dame schools and small church schools, there was no common system of education. Many poor children would have only had access to education at Sunday School, or possibly would have had no education at all. By the end of the period, a state system had been set up and it was compulsory for all children to attend one sort of school or another.

## Introduction
● Find out what the children already know about the following question: *What was it like in Victorian schools?*
● Explain that in this lesson, they are going to find out what lessons were like in the Board schools which were set up for all children in the late Victorian period.
● Ask the children what they know about how teaching was carried out, how good behaviour was maintained and what sort of things were learned in lessons.
● Discuss the strict manner of the teacher, the use of corporal punishment, the emphasis of instruction and rote-learning and the conformity demanded of the children.

## Main teaching activity
● Provide the class with some examples of Victorian lessons, such as the one on religious instruction on the photocopiable sheet on page 99.
● Set up the classroom as if in Victorian times, with the children seated in rows, sitting up straight and all facing the front.
● If possible, use props, such as old-fashioned clothes, a mortar board and gown, an old-fashioned teacher's chair and a cane.
● Carry out a role play, using a Victorian lesson (for example using the photocopiable sheet 'A Victorian lesson' on page 99), and taking into account the expectations common in Victorian times, for example, with reference to behaviour. Insist on total silence, carry out a 'hand inspection' and demand that all the children produce identical pieces of work.
● Following the role-play activity, set the class, working in pairs, the task of writing a short playscript of a Victorian classroom.

## Plenary
● Ask the children how they enjoyed their 'Victorian lesson'. Discuss whether this was a better or worse way of teaching than they have today. Talk about how and why things have changed.

## Differentiation
Provide additional adult support for the less able writers as they write their playscript.

# Comparing Victorian and present-day schools

## Objectives
● To use dates and vocabulary relating to the passing of time.
● To know about characteristic features of the period and societies studied.
● To identify and describe reasons for, and results of, historical events, situations and changes in the periods studied.

## Vocabulary
master, logbooks, monitors, slates, inkwells

## Resources
Art materials and paper; pictures and written sources about school life in the past; extracts from Victorian literature, such as *David Copperfield* by Charles Dickens (Penguin Classics). Useful websites include www.woodlands-junior.kent.sch.uk/Homework/victorians.html

## Links
NC English KS2: En1 (3) to talk effectively as members of a group.
NC Art and design KS2: (2c) to use a variety of methods and approaches to communicate observations.

## Background
Many things were similar to present-day primary schools in the Board Schools. There was, as today, a clear curriculum, dominated by reading, writing and arithmetic. There was religious instruction and holidays of a similar length to today. Possibly the most significant difference was in the type of behaviour management used. Corporal punishment was considered good for a child's development ('spare the rod and spoil the child') and school was not expected to be a place for fun! Resources were generally scarce, and children were only provided with a reading book after they had mastered some of the rudiments of reading through whole-class teaching on the blackboard.

## Introduction
● Explain the lesson objectives to the class.
● Tell them that they will need to answer the question: *How is school different now from school in Victorian times?*

## Main teaching activity
● Look at pictures and other sources about Victorian schools. Ask the children to note key features in these sources and to compare them with present-day schools, for example: the size of classes, the way the classrooms are organised and so on.
● Discuss with the children the changes that have taken place in school life since Victorian times.
● Encourage them to think of reasons for these changes, for example: better resources, different ideas about the purposes of education, changing attitudes about what boys and girls will go on to do, and so on.
● Organise the class to work in pairs: one child making a picture focusing on a detail of Victorian school life, and the other a comparative modern one. The children can use a variety of art media and styles for their work.

## Plenary
● Make a display of the pictures and review the changes that they show.

## Differentiation
Organise the class to work in mixed ability pairs to provide support for the less able children.

# How rich and poor children spent their time

### Objectives
● To know about characteristic features of the period and societies studied.
● To know about the social, cultural, religious and ethnic diversity of the societies studied, in Britain and the wider world.
● To find out about events, people and changes studied from visual sources.

### Vocabulary
mines, factories, inspector, supervisor, machinery

### Resources
Illustrations, contemporary engravings and pictures showing poor children in the streets or at work; portraits of wealthy children playing, reading books, at school and so on; writing materials.

### Links
NLS Y6 T1 Text 14: to develop skills of autobiographical writing in role.
NC English KS2: En1 (3) to talk effectively as members of a group.

## Background

The lives of rich and poor children differed greatly throughout the Victorian period. While those from wealthy backgrounds grew up well-fed and clean, with access to doctors when needed and comfortable homes and toys to play with, their poorer contemporaries would not have enjoyed these comforts. They would have lived in overcrowded, damp homes, either small cottages in the countryside, or back-to-back houses urban areas. They would have had poor clothing, often wearing 'hand-me-downs' from older siblings. Food would have been scarce and there would have been very few toys, other than homemade ones. There are excellent descriptions of this contrast in *The Water Babies* by Charles Kingsley (Award Publications) and in many of Dickens' novels.

## Introduction

● Discuss the differences between the lives of rich and poor children today, for example: Do the poor children go to school? Do they work? Do they have enough to eat? Do they have books to read?
● Explain the lesson objectives to the class and tell the children that they are going to look at the following question: *How did the lives of rich and poor children compare in Victorian times?*

## Main teaching activity

● Provide illustrations and pictures showing poor children at work in the mines and in factories, sweeping chimneys and so on, or in the streets; and then portraits of wealthy children playing, reading books or attending private schools.
● Talk about what a day in the life of each type of child would have been like.
● Look at the drawings of children at work in the mines and ask the class to think about what it must have been like.
● Look at illustrations of public schools, and discuss the sort of children that would have attended these. Ask the children what sort of jobs they think these children would have done when they left school, compared with the poor.
● Ask the class to write diary entries for a day in the life of a rich or poor child.

## Plenary

● Review the diary entries the children have written and then set them the task of writing a diary entry for their own day, as homework.

## Differentiation

Support less able writers with starter sentences for their diary entries.

# Leisure time

## Objectives
● To find out about the events, people and changes studied from a variety of sources of information.
● To recall, select and organise historical information.
● To communicate their knowledge and understanding of history in a variety of ways.

## Vocabulary
leisure time, railway fares

## Resources
Pictures and accounts of fêtes, seaside holidays, day trips to the countryside; lists of fares and railway timetables from books and websites, such as http://www.learningcurve.gov.uk/snapshots and http://tofino.ex.ac.uk/virvic/themes/leisure/home.htm

## Links
NLS Y5 T1 Text 26: to make notes for different purposes.
NC Art and design KS2: (2c) to use a variety of methods and approaches to communicate observations.

## Background
As public transport began to develop, especially in the form of the railways, people's leisure time began to change. The usual village fairs and fêtes continued to take place on holidays, with maypole dancing, stalls and games. However, increasingly in the later Victorian period, trips to the countryside or to the seaside grew in popularity among all levels of society in the towns. It became fashionable, and was considered good for the health, to spend time at the seaside. The new railway system made this sort of travel a fairly affordable possibility for many as it had never been before. More people travelled to London, using the newly created, cheap day-return tickets on the trains, to see the Great Exhibition at the Crystal Palace than attended the Millennium Dome at the beginning of the 21st century.

## Introduction
● Ask the children what they like to do when they have a day off school. Discuss all their favourite things, especially what they do in the long summer holidays.
● Ask if anyone knows what the Victorians did and explain that, in this lesson, they are going to find out about the following question: *What did Victorians do in their spare time?*

## Main teaching activity
● Give the class sources from Victorian times, such as pictures and accounts of fêtes, seaside holidays, day trips to the countryside, lists of fares and railway timetables to study.
● Discuss these with the children, encouraging them to make inferences from what they have seen and to identify the key features of Victorian leisure.
● Make a list of these features on the board or whiteboard for the children to refer to.
● Organise the class to work in pairs and set them the task of designing the front page of a magazine on 'A great day out on your May Day holiday'. The page needs to contain illustrations and captions. Encourage the children to try to use Victorian styles in their drawing and writing.

## Plenary
● Display the children's work and discuss the features they have illustrated and how well they have captured the styles used in Victorian times.

## Differentiation
Organise the class to work in mixed ability pairs to provide support for the less able children. Provide adult support as necessary in the writing activity.

# Church and Sunday school

## Objectives
● To know about characteristic features of the period and societies studied.
● To find out about the events, people and changes studied from a variety of sources of information.
● To ask and answer questions, and to select and record information relevant to the focus of the enquiry.

## Vocabulary
Sunday school, monitor, instructor

## Resources
Variety of sources showing Victorians in or going to church in their 'Sunday best', for example from websites such as http://www.request.org.uk/main/history/victorians/victorians08.htm; if possible, a visit to a re-enactment of a Sunday school.

## Links
NC English KS2: En1 (3) to talk effectively as members of a group; (4a) to create, adapt and sustain different roles, individually and in groups. NC PSHE & citizenship KS2: (4b) to think about the lives of people living in other places and times, and people with different values and customs.

## Background
Going to church and to Sunday school, if you were a child, was an essential feature of life in Victorian times. There were many religious denominations and there was strong growth in the Protestant non-conformist churches, such as the Methodists and Baptists. This led to some rivalry and a determined effort in the Anglican Church to extend their influence, including through a programme of cathedral building. However, whatever particular creed you believed in, by the late Victorian period, it was essential to attend church every week. Apart from religious conviction, going to church was a social obligation. It was an occasion to dress up in your 'Sunday best' and to be seen as affluent and successful by your neighbours. There was competition about who looked the smartest each week. Social customs were very important to the Victorians, and so weddings and funerals were extremely important occasions, again, linked with attending church.

## Introduction
● Explain to the class that in this lesson they are going to think about the question: *What were Sundays like in Victorian times?*

## Main teaching activity
● Ask the class what sort of things they often do on a Sunday.
● Show the children a variety of sources showing Victorians in or going to church in their 'Sunday best'.
● Discuss what the sources suggest happened on Sundays in Victorian times.
● Talk about the importance of going to church in Victorian times and the importance of being seen at church.
● Explain how many poorer children, who had to work during the week, had to go to school on Sundays, and that this was the only education many of them ever had. Talk about how much they could have learned at these schools. (If possible, arrange a visit to a re-enactment of a Sunday school.)
● Act in role as the teacher at church or chapel and re-enact part of a typical Sunday school experience with the class. Adopt a very strict manner, not allowing any children to speak or turn round. Inspect the children's appearance and hands for cleanliness, then read prayers and Bible stories, give moral instruction, sing hymns and so on.

## Plenary
● Talk about Sunday school today and find out if any children go to a Sunday school, or to a school associated with other religions outside their normal school hours, for example, Jewish or Islamic classes.

## Differentiation
Direct appropriate questions to children of differing abilities.

# Changes for children in Victorian times

## Objectives
● To ask and answer questions, and to select and record information relevant to the focus of the enquiry.
● To identify and describe reasons for, and results of, historical events, situations and changes in the periods studied.
● To find out about the events, people and changes studied from a variety of sources of information.

## Vocabulary
change, continuity, poverty, reign

## Resources
The photocopiable sheets 'Victorian Britain' on page100, one per child, and 'Timeline of Victorian Britain' on page 95, one copy enlarged for class work; pictures of poor children from the beginning of Victoria's reign and similar from the end (useful websites include www.richard-york.co.uk/past/vicchildren.html).

## Links
NLS Y5 T1 Text 26: to make notes for different purposes; Y6 T1 Text 16: to use the styles and conventions of journalism. NC English KS2: En1 (3) to talk effectively as members of a group.

## Background
The pace of change in Victorian Britain was rapid. The most obvious change was the introduction of compulsory schooling, however, this was only applicable at the 'elementary' stage . There was little opportunity for working people to attend secondary, further or higher education. There were slow but gradual improvements in housing and working conditions for the working classes. Real changes, however, often lagged far behind what appeared in principle. Similarly, there was little change to provision of health care for individuals unless they could afford to pay for it.

## Introduction
● Talk about the big changes that took place between the beginning of Victoria's reign and the end (1837-1901). (Use the photocopiable sheet 'Timeline of Victorian Britain' on page 95.)
● Explain that they are going to consider the question: *How much did all this change actually affect the everyday lives of children?*

## Main teaching activity
● Ask the children to compare the scenes on the photocopiable sheet 'Victorian Britain' on page 100.
● Encourage the children to say what changes took place during Victorian times, such as the change from young children working in mines and factories to attending school.
● Discuss with the class why they think the changes took place. For example: the increasing wealth of the country as a whole; shock amongst the middle classes when they learned of the plight of poor children; the work of a few reformers and politicians.
● Talk about whether children's lives really changed very much, for example: What happened if poor children were ill? Did poor children have electric lights in their homes? Are new inventions and developments more likely to have affected richer children?
● Set up a debate between those who have opposing views, concluding with a vote to decide what the majority view is.
● During the debate, ask the children to make notes as if journalists and then write up a brief newspaper report.

## Plenary
● Conclude by discussing the changes that have taken place since 1901, for example: the chance of higher education for all, the national health service, support for people out of work and so on.

## Differentiation
Differentiate by asking questions appropriate to ability.

# What do we know now about the Victorians?

## Objectives
● To identify and describe reasons for, and results of, historical events, situations and changes in the periods studied.
● To recall, select and organise historical information.
● To communicate their knowledge and understanding of history in a variety of ways.

## Vocabulary
all the vocabulary from the topic

## Resources
Charts for the answers to the quiz.

## Background
This lesson provide the opportunity for an enjoyable conclusion to work on the Victorians. It is designed in the form of a quiz, which could be played either as a team game or, as is suggested here, as an individual quiz for assessment purposes. To assess children's skills and understanding of historical concepts, ongoing observation will have been needed during the previous lessons. However, this individual game will allow a final assessment of each child's factual knowledge.

## Introduction
● Explain to the class that they are going to work on the question: *What do we know now about the Victorians?* by holding a class quiz.

## Main teaching activity
● Organise the children for a class quiz. Provide each child with a simple chart for putting down their answers. Explain that these can be in any form as long as they are clear to the reader.
● Devise a series of questions based on the topics studied, such as key dates and personalities of the period, key changes that took place, major events, characteristic features of the period, such as church-going, dress and so on. Questions might include:

> Who set up homes for destitute and orphaned boys and girls?
> In which year did Queen Victoria marry Albert?
> *David Copperfield* and *Oliver Twist* were written by which famous author?
> When was the Great Exhibition at the Crystal Palace?
> What was the title of Charles Darwin's most famous book and what was it about?
> Give two changes that took place in Victorian Britain that would have affected children.
> What was the Reform Act of 1867?
> Where did Florence Nightingale go to nurse soldiers in hospital?
> Where would most Victorian children go on Sunday?
> What document might you use to dsicover how many people lived in a particular house?

● Use the children's answers to assess their factual knowledge and understanding of the Victorian period. When marking, give credit for information that the children may have found out independently.

## Plenary
● Hold a whole-class review of the answers to the quiz.

## Differentiation
Include questions at a variety of levels of difficulty.

## Links
NLS Y5 T1 Text 26: to make notes for different purposes.

# Timeline of Victorian Britain

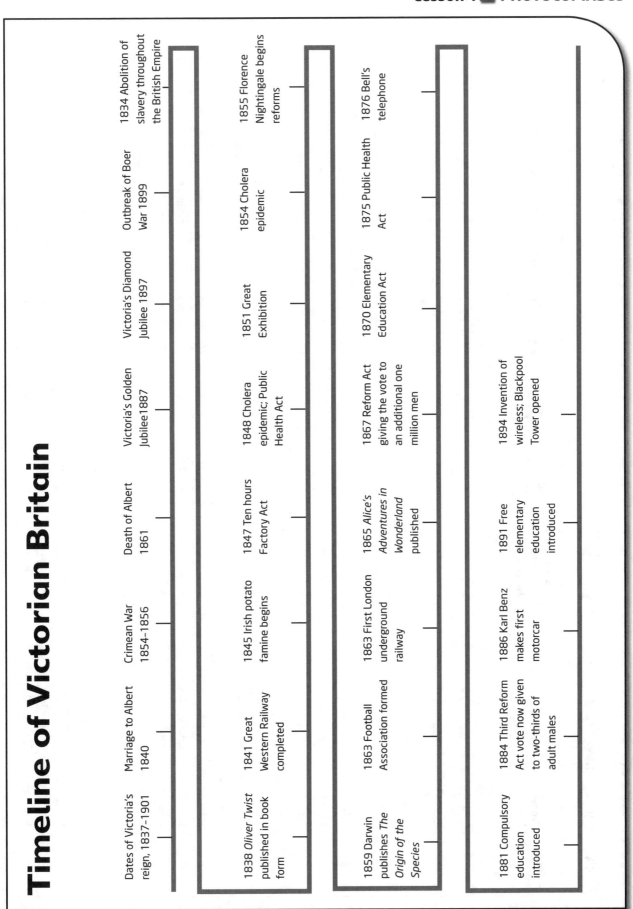

Dates of Victoria's reign, 1837–1901

Marriage to Albert 1840

Crimean War 1854–1856

Death of Albert 1861

Victoria's Golden Jubilee 1887

Victoria's Diamond Jubilee 1897

Outbreak of Boer War 1899

1834 Abolition of slavery throughout the British Empire

1838 *Oliver Twist* published in book form

1841 Great Western Railway completed

1845 Irish potato famine begins

1847 Ten hours Factory Act

1848 Cholera epidemic; Public Health Act

1851 Great Exhibition

1854 Cholera epidemic

1855 Florence Nightingale begins reforms

1859 Darwin publishes *The Origin of the Species*

1863 Football Association formed

1863 First London underground railway

1865 *Alice's Adventures in Wonderland* published

1867 Reform Act giving the vote to an additional one million men

1870 Elementary Education Act

1875 Public Health Act

1876 Bell's telephone

1881 Compulsory education introduced

1884 Third Reform Act vote now given to two-thirds of adult males

1886 Karl Benz makes first motorcar

1891 Free elementary education introduced

1894 Invention of wireless; Blackpool Tower opened

# Census extract 1: 1851

| House number | Street | Name | Relationship to head of household | Marital status | Male/ Female | Age | Occupation | Place of birth |
|---|---|---|---|---|---|---|---|---|
| 9 | John Street | Mary Leek | head | W | f | 45 | n/s | Newton, Lancs. |
| 9 | John Street | Edward Leek | son | U | m | 18 | hawker | Cheetham, Lancs. |
| 9 | John Street | Thomas Leek | son | U | m | 16 | painter | Cheetham, Lancs. |
| 9 | John Street | Mary Leek | daughter | U | f | 11 | silk winder | Cheetham, Lancs. |
| 9 | John Street | Thomas Leek | son | U | m | 7 | scholar | Cheetham, Lancs. |
| 8 | John Street | Holden Hayes | head | M | m | 39 | bleacher | Middleton, Lancs. |
| 8 | John Street | Sarah Hayes | wife | M | f | 38 | n/s | Manchester |
| 8 | John Street | Miriam Hayes | daughter | U | f | 15 | power loom weaver | Manchester |
| 8 | John Street | Ann Hayes | daughter | U | f | 3 | n/s | Manchester |
| 8 | John Street | Mary Ann Pollitt | lodger | U | f | 13 | power loom weaver | Manchester |
| 7 | John Street | George Coulstone | head | M | m | 40 | glazier | Poland, Warsaw |
| 7 | John Street | Nancy Coulstone | wife | M | f | 32 | n/s | Poland, Warsaw |
| 7 | John Street | Harriet Coulstone | daughter | U | f | 1 | n/s | Poland, Warsaw |
| 7 | John Street | Mary Ann Coulstone | daughter | U | f | 4mn | n/s | Manchester |
| 7 | John Street | Mary Flanaghan | servant | U | f | 15 | servant | Ireland |
| 6 | John Street | Charles McCardy | head | M | m | 36 | dyer | Manchester |
| 6 | John Street | Ellen McCardy | wife | M | f | 28 | cap maker | Oldham, Lancs. |
| 6 | John Street | James McCardy | son | U | m | 15 | dyer | Clayton, Lancs. |
| 6 | John Street | Martha McCardy | daughter | U | f | 7 | scholar | Manchester |
| 6 | John Street | Robert McCardy | son | U | m | 5 | scholar | Manchester |
| 6 | John Street | Sarah McCardy | daughter | U | f | 2 | n/s | Manchester |
| 5 | John Street | Charles Cumberbirch | head | M | m | 30 | doll maker | Ches. Stockport |
| 5 | John Street | Ellen Cumberbirch | wife | M | f | 24 | n/s | Manchester |
| 5 | John Street | Eliza Cumberbirch | daughter | U | f | 1 | n/s | Manchester |

📕SCHOLASTIC

100 HISTORY LESSONS: Ages 7–11

# Census extract 2: 1881

| Street/House | Forename | Surname | Relationship to head of household | Marital status | Gender | Age | Occupation | Birthplace |
|---|---|---|---|---|---|---|---|---|
| Didsbury Park | Hannah Maria | DOOLEY | Servant (Head) | U | Female | 24 | Housemaid domestic servant | Ladybarn, Lancashire, England |
| Didsbury Park | Phoebe | JACKSON | Servant | U | Female | 32 | Cook domestic servant | Milton, Oxford, England |
| Didsbury Park | Margaret | ROBERTS | Servant (Head) | U | Female | 47 | Cook domestic servant | St Asaph, Flint, Wales |
| Didsbury Park | Aruchia | BECKTON | Head | W | Female | 40 | Allowance from my father | Manchester, Lancashire, England |
| Didsbury Park | Aruchia C. | BECKTON | Daughter | U | Female | 15 | Scholar | Didsbury, Lancashire, England |
| Didsbury Park | Ernest | BECKTON | Son | U | Male | 14 | Scholar | Didsbury, Lancashire, England |
| Didsbury Park | Margaret A. | BECKTON | Daughter | U | Female | 9 | Scholar | Didsbury, Lancashire, England |
| Didsbury Park | Edith Mary | BECKTON | Daughter | U | Female | 6 | Scholar | Didsbury, Lancashire, England |
| Didsbury Park | Maud Josephine | BECKTON | Daughter | U | Female | 5 | | Manchester, Lancashire, England |
| Didsbury Park | Gertrude Lilian | BECKTON | Daughter | U | Female | 4 | | Manchester, Lancashire, England |
| Didsbury Park | Ann D. | HINDER | Servant | U | Female | 44 | Governess | Depl Ashton, Wiltshire, England |
| Didsbury Park | Mary | LIGHTFOOT | Servant | W | Female | 46 | Cook | Manchester, Lancashire, England |
| Didsbury Park | Harriet Anne | MARSHALL | Servant | U | Female | 24 | Nurse | Doncaster, York, England |
| Didsbury Park | Richard Edward | LIGHTFOOT | Servant | U | Male | 20 | Butler (F S) | Nantwich, Cheshire, England |

# Lord Shaftesbury and Dr Barnado

### Lord Shaftesbury

Born in 1801, Lord Shaftesbury came from a wealthy family. First he attended boarding school and then went to Oxford to study, an opportunity only open to the rich in Victorian times. At the age of twenty-five, he became a Member of Parliament, and it was when he was working in Parliament that he saw reports on child labour. He was so horrified at what he read that he became concerned about the lives of the poor, and of poor children in particular. In 1832 he became leader of the Factory Reform Movement in the House of Commons, stopping factories employing young children. He found this role very difficult at times, and he had many critics, who said he was not really interested in the poor but just wanted to attack the mill owners. They said that he took up the factory question 'as much from a dislike of the mill owners as sympathy with the mill workers'. He was a strictly-brought-up Victorian, refined, thoughtful and highly educated. Lord Shaftesbury died in 1885, after a lifetime of work on behalf of the poor.

### Dr Barnardo

Dr Thomas Barnardo was a similar kind of philanthropist to Lord Shaftesbury, but he used different methods to address the problems of the poor. Born in Dublin in 1845, into quite poor circumstances, he worked as an Evangelical preacher for a while before moving to London and studying medicine. He had to work very hard to achieve what he wanted, unlike those born into wealthy families. Barnardo soon began to see the plight of the poor and homeless children in the city and set up a Ragged School. While making a speech about this problem, he was heard by Lord Shaftesbury and by Robert Barclay, a banker, and both men were so impressed with his ideas that they agreed to support him in his desire to help these children. He was then able to set up homes for orphaned and destitute boys and girls, where they were well cared for and received a full education. His homes continued well into the 20th century. Dr Barnardo died in 1905.

# A Victorian lesson

◼ Read Genesis chapters seven and eight together as a class.

◼ The teacher reads out the questions, to which the children respond with the answers (in italics).

## THE FLOOD

1. For how long did God cause it to rain when the flood came?
*For forty days and forty nights.*

2. How high did the flood rise?
*It covered the tops of the hills and drowned everyone except those in the Ark.*

3. What became of the Ark?
*It floated about on the water.*

4. Where did the Ark rest when the water began to go down?
*On Mount Ararat.*

5. What did Noah send out of the Ark when he thought the water was nearly gone?
*A raven and a dove.*

6. What became of them?
*The raven flew away but the dove came back to the Ark.*

7. How did Noah know that the flood was over?
*He sent out the dove again and she brought back an olive leaf.*
*(This showed Noah that the trees were in leaf again.)*

8. What did Noah do as soon as he came out of the Ark?
*He built an altar and offered a sacrifice\* to God.*

9. What did God promise Noah?
*That he would never send another flood to drown all the world.*

10. What did God show Noah as a token of His promise?
*A rainbow.*

*\*By a sacrifice is meant something offered or given to God as Cain offered fruit. Noah took the beasts and fowls, which he offered to God, killed them and burnt them on the altar. He did this to show how thankful he was to God for saving him and his family from the flood. We may learn from Noah's example, that we, like him, should never forget to thank God for His mercies to us, more especially after He has delivered us from some great danger or trouble.*

# Victorian Britain

Children at school (Late Victorian)

Fish seller (Early Victorian)

Street sweeper (Early Victorian)

# CHAPTER 6

# Ancient Greeks

The modern world owes much to the beliefs, achievements and legacies of Ancient Greece. The Ancient Greeks left behind a wealth of literature, drama, philosophy, science and mathematics. Ideas, theories and practices in constant use today are often rooted in Greek principles – such as the Hippocratic oath, classical architectural styles and events including the Olympic Games. Amazingly accurate Greek maps were used in later times by explorers such as Christopher Columbus. We still read and enjoy Greek myths and legends. Not least, of course, are the many influences on languages across the Western world derived from Greek. A study of Ancient Greece also provides excellent opportunities for children to note similarities and differences with their own lives, change, and also the high degree of continuity with the present day. It is also helpful that modern-day Greece will be familiar to many children as it is a popular tourist destination.

|  | OBJECTIVES | MAIN ACTIVITY |
|---|---|---|
| **Lesson 1** | To recall, select and organise historical information.<br>To communicate their knowledge in a variety of ways. | Children discuss what they already know about Greece and what they would like to know about Ancient Greece. |
| **Lesson 2** ▯ | To use dates and vocabulary relating to the passing of time.<br>To recall, select and organise historical information. | Children study maps of modern and Ancient Greece and work on a general historical timeline. |
| **Lesson 3** ▯ | To place events, people and changes into correct periods of time.<br>To use dates and historical vocabulary to describe the period studied. | Children create a timeline for Ancient Greece and research particular events. |
| **Lesson 4** ▯ | To know about social, cultural, religious and ethnic diversity. | Through role play, children learn about city-states. |
| **Lesson 5** | To know about characteristic features of the period studied.<br>To know about social, cultural, religious and ethnic diversity of societies studied. | Using role play and debate, children learn how democracy worked in Ancient Greece. |
| **Lesson 6** | To find out about the past from a variety of sources. | Children learn about the roles of men, women and children in Ancient Greece. |
| **Lesson 7** ▯ | To find out about the past from a variety of sources. | Children research Pythagoras and other famous scholars. |
| **Lesson 8** ▯ | To know about characteristic features of the period studied.<br>To recognise that the past is represented and interpreted in different ways.<br>To find out about the past from visual sources and accounts. | Using the Battle of Marathon as an example, children learn about bias in historical accounts. |
| **Lesson 9** ▯ | To know about characteristic features of the period studied.<br>To find out about the past from visual sources and accounts. | Children research the history of the Olympic Games. |
| **Lesson 10** ▯ | To know about characteristic features of the period studied.<br>To find out about the past from visual and written sources. | Children study Ancient Greek drama and create masks. |
| **Lesson 11** ▯ | To find out about the past from a variety of sources. | Children read about Alexander the Great, consider other heroes of Ancient Greece and write playscripts. |
| **Lesson 12** | To recall, select and organise historical information.<br>To communicate their knowledge in a variety of ways. | Children consider how ideas from Ancient Greece have influenced modern thinking. |
| **Lesson 13** | To recall, select and organise historical information.<br>To communicate their knowledge in a variety of ways. | A guidebook to Ancient Greece is completed by the whole class. |

# What do we know about modern and Ancient Greece?

## Objectives
● To recall, select and organise historical information.
● To communicate their knowledge and understanding of history in a variety of ways.

## Vocabulary
modern, state, Ancient, empire

## Resources
Postcards and holiday brochures about Greece; pictures and photographs from books and the internet, such as www.greeklandscapes.com/photoscapes/index.html, www.tours2greece.info/greece-travel/photo_gallery.php and www.worldphotolocations.com

## Links
NLS Y5 T1 Text 26: to make notes for different purposes.
NC English KS2: En1 (3) to talk effectively as members of a group.

## Background
By this stage in their school lives, many children will have learned some information about Ancient Greece, in some cases, a surprising amount. It can be very useful, as an initial activity, to find out how much children already know. This can help inform the choice of subsequent themes and activities. There is so much written and so much information about life in Ancient Greece that, even those children who may have already learned a significant amount, perhaps at home, will find much more to interest them. This activity should be done at the start of studying the Ancient Greeks. At the end of the whole topic as an assessment task, the children review or reinforce their learning by making a 'guidebook'.

## Introduction
● Explain that this topic is going to be about how people lived and the key events in the Ancient Greek city-states and Empire.
● Ask the children what they know about modern-day Greece.

## Main teaching activity
● Ask the children if anyone has been to Greece.
● Look at resources about Greece in modern times.
● Discuss what the children already know about Greece.
● Ask what they think people about to go there would like to know about the country's history, and make a list of questions.
● Talk about how the history of Ancient Greece is always fascinating for visitors, and how this is one of the most famous things about Greece.
● Explain that, by the end of the topic, the class will have created a guide for tourists, which focuses on Ancient Greeks and their lives.
● Divide the class into suitable working groups and give each group the task of devising a different chapter to complete by the end of the topic, by finding out, from lessons and their own research, answers to their original questions.
● Ask the groups to make notes of their questions and of the way they plan to organise their chapter, what the contents might be and who is responsible for each item. They will work on the chapter contents over the course of the whole topic.

## Plenary
● Review, comment upon and amend each group's plans.

## Differentiation
Organise the class to work in mixed ability groups to provide support for the less able children.

# Modern and Ancient Greece

## Objectives
● To use dates and vocabulary relating to the passing of time.
● To recall, select and organise historical information.
● To ask and answer questions, and to select and record information relevant to the focus of the enquiry.

## Vocabulary
Mediterranean, Aegean, Athens

## Resources
Map of modern Greece; globe of the world; general class timeline, showing years BC and ad, up to the present day; cards with dates of major historical events, such as the Tudor period and the Second World War; blank cards; the photocopiable sheet 'Map of Ancient Greece' on page 115, one per child; reference resources on places in Ancient Greece; coloured pencils.

## Links
NC Geography KS2: (1a) to ask geographical questions; (2a) to use appropriate geographical vocabulary; (2c) to use atlases and globes, and maps and plans at a range of scales.

## Background
The history and geography of Greece link it with both the West and the East. For many centuries in modern times, Greece was ruled by the Byzantine Empire with its capital in Constantinople (now Istanbul). Greece also lies partly in the Aegean and partly in the Mediterranean seas. This lesson aims to help children know about the location of Greece in the world and also its place in history, so that they will have a good contextual understanding of themes that they will cover during the topic.

## Introduction
● Explain the lesson objectives and prompt the children to become involved in the enquiry by asking questions such as: *Where was Ancient Greece? When was Ancient Greece?*

## Main teaching activity
● On a general class timeline, locate the Ancient Greek period (c2000BC–c146AD).
● Revise the children's understanding of BC and AD.
● Give out the cards showing the dates of major historical events and ask the children to work together to place them on the class timeline.
● Let the children have some blank cards to fill in some dates and events of their own choosing. For example, they may wish to put on the timeline the birth of Christ or some very recent historical events.
● Show the children a globe of the world and ask the children to locate Greece on it.
● Display a map of modern-day Greece and ask the children to locate important cities, such as Athens, the major islands and seas. If any of the children have been on holiday to Greece, they may be able to indicate these places to you on the map also.
● Give each child a copy of the photocopiable 'Map of Ancient Greece' on page 115. Discuss it with the children and ask them if there are any similarities or differences.
● Hand out some coloured pencils and ask the children to colour the towns, cities and seas, completing the labels.

## Plenary
● Discuss why we still remember the Ancient Greeks.

## Differentiation
Provide adult support as necessary in the map-work activity.

# Timeline of Ancient Greece

## Objectives
● To place events, people and changes into correct periods of time.
● To use dates and historical vocabulary to describe the period studied.

## Vocabulary
Crete, Minoan, Trojan, Persian, Peloponesian

## Resources
Timeline covering the period of Ancient Greece; key dates on cards (see the teaching activity); the photocopiable sheet 'Map of Ancient Greece' on page 115, if possible completed in Lesson 2; resource packs and books (for example: *Ancient Greece* by Andrew Solway (Oxford University Press) and *Ancient Greece* (Eyewitness Books) by Anne Pearson (DK Publishing)); internet resources on Ancient Greece, including key events of the period, for example: www.bbc.co.uk/schools/ancientgreece and www.ancientgreece.co.uk/menu.html

## Links
NLS Y5 T1 Text 26: to make notes for different purposes.
NC Geography KS2: (2c) to use atlases and globes, and maps and plans at a range of scales.
NC ICT KS2: (1a) to talk about what information they need and how they can find and use it.

## Background
This lesson uses a timeline to enable children to understand the long period of history involved in the study of Ancient Greece and to start to place specific, important events in chronological order. Older children are likely to have an initial understanding of how to date events that take place in the years before Christ, but this activity will help to consolidate that understanding. Some children will be beginning to comprehend the significance of dates, but they are still likely to need considerable support. For this reason, the assembling of information on the class timeline is suggested as a whole-class activity, where the teacher can observe, prompt and support children.

## Introduction
● Explain how the period of time when the Ancient Greeks ruled was very long, lasting for more than 2000 years.
● Compare this with the modern period we now live in.
● Tell the class that in this lesson they will be finding out about some of the key events that happened during the Ancient Greek period.

## Main teaching activity
● Show the children your timeline covering the Ancient Greek period (c2000BC– c146BC). If appropriate, refer back to your general historical timeline from Lesson 1 on page 103.
● Give the children a set of cards with key dates and events such as:

c2000BC Palace of Knossos built on Crete, during Cretan rule over Greece
c1400BC destruction of Minoan culture
750BC Homer born and the mythology of the Trojan Wars subsequently written
776BC first Olympic Games
490BC Battle of Marathon
431–404BC Peloponesian Wars (Athens /Sparta)
c146BC Romans conquer Greece.

● If appropriate, refer to the photocopiable sheet 'Map of Ancient Greece' on page 115, which the children completed in Lesson 2. Help them find where events took place on the map, for example, Marathon.
● Organise the class into groups and allocate them one of the items on the timeline to research, using internet and book resources.

## Plenary
● The children could make a timeline on the computer - adding details, maps, photos and so on found online. Alternatively, ask the children to place their findings, shown as labels or illustrations, on the timeline.

## Differentiation
Working in mixed ability groups will provide support for the less able.

# Athens and Sparta

## Objectives
● To know about the social, cultural, religious and ethnic diversity of the societies studied, in Britain and the wider world.

## Vocabulary
Athens, Sparta, spartan

## Resources
The completed photocopiable sheet 'Map of Ancient Greece' on page 115, or another similar map; 'thinking' cards (see Main teaching activity).

## Links
NC PSHE & citizenship KS2: (2a) to research, discuss and debate topical issues, problems and events; (4b) to think about the lives of people living in other places and times, and people with different beliefs and customs. NC Geography KS2: (2c) to use atlases and globes, and maps and plans at a range of scales. NC English KS2: En1 (3) to talk effectively as members of a group; (4a) to create, adapt and sustain different roles, individually and in groups.

## Background
Ancient Greece was made up of over 50 different 'city-states', called in Greek the 'polis'. These were self-governing communities, centred around a large town or city. They were social, political, religious and economic centres and each citizen felt a sense of identity related to his own city-state, rather like a very large, extended family. There were, therefore, people who regarded themselves as 'Athenians' or 'Spartans' and they prided themselves on their sometimes very different traditions and ways of life. Each city-state was independent and managed its own affairs, including the maintenance of an army for its own defence. City-states sometimes went to war with each other, as in the case of the war between Athens and Sparta, known as the Peloponesian War.

## Introduction
● Refer to the map of Ancient Greece and note where Athens and Sparta were. Talk about their different traditions, and how they were organised as 'city-states'.
● Explain that this meant that they governed themselves as separate states, often in conflict with each other.
● Discuss the lesson objectives and talk about how there were different ideas, beliefs and cultures even within one country, in the past. Tell the class that they are going to consider the questions: *How were Athens and Sparta different?* and *How did city-states work?*

## Main teaching activity
● Tell the class that they are going to 'become' two city-states.
● Divide the class into two and tell them that each group is one city, but that they do not have anyone to rule them or organise them.
● Give out a number of 'thinking' cards. These might include the following: *How will the state be governed? What will people need to live comfortably in this city-state? How will food be provided? How will they defend themselves from attack? What if some people or groups will not cooperate?*
● Give the children a fixed amount of time to decide what they must do and then call them together to discuss their decisions.
● Have both groups approached the problems in the same way? Do they both have the same priorities?

## Plenary
● Given children five to ten minutes to set up their 'governments'. Discuss what sorts of jobs might need to be done. Have both city-states set themselves up in the same way?

## Differentiation
Provide support and ensure that all children take part in the role play.

# Ancient Greek democracy

## Background

The Ancient Greeks are renowned for their democracies, which were the political systems used to manage the governments of most of the city-states. However, the Greek notion of democracy was very different from that we understand today. The Ancient Greeks did not consider slaves or women to be full citizens of the state, as in many ways they were not, since they lacked many basic freedoms. These two groups, therefore, had no place in Greek democracy and did not have the vote. Only free men participated in this form of democracy. Care may be needed in this lesson if there are children from different cultural backgrounds in the class, perhaps where the role of women in society is still a current issue.

## Introduction

● Explain to the class that in this lesson they are going to learn about the idea of 'democracy', how this is originally a word from Greek, and how Ancient Greek democracy is different from our modern version.
● Briefly discuss the children's idea of what democracy is, and give a simple explanation if necessary.

## Main teaching activity

● Explain that they are going to re-enact a democratic event that might have taken place in Ancient Greece.
● Tell the class that they are living in an Ancient Greek city-state, which is democratically run.
● Provide a simulated situation for the children to resolve in their new role as 'governors' of the city-state, for example: there is a threat of war from another city-state nearby and they need to decide what to do; one governor wants women to be allowed to come out of their homes and help with running the state because there will not be enough men to do this if there is a war; a governor wants girls to be allowed to go to school.
● Organise some of the boys in two opposing groups at the front of the classroom. Tell the boys who are not in these two groups that they are slaves and not entitled to have any say in government. Tell the girls to 'stay at home' at the back of the classroom.
● Ask the boys at the front to debate the issue, staying in role.

## Plenary

● Conclude with a vote and a discussion about the process of democracy in Ancient Greece. Talk about whether it really was democracy or not in the children's opinion. Consider why society in Ancient Greece was organised in this way. How did the children who were not allowed to take part in the debate feel about the process?

## Differentiation

Differentiate the questions according to individual needs in the class.

## Objectives
● To know about characteristic features of the period and societies studied.
● To know about the social, cultural, religious and ethnic diversity of the societies studied, in Britain and the wider world.

## Vocabulary
democracy, democratic, city-state, governor

## Resources
A simulated situation for the children to resolve (see Main teaching activity).

## Links
NC Citizenship KS2: (1a) to explain their views, on issues that affect themselves and society; (2g) to know what democracy is.
NC English KS2: En1 (3) to talk effectively as members of a group; (4a) to create, adapt and sustain different roles, individually and in groups.

# Homes and families

## Objectives
● To find out about the events, people and changes studied from an appropriate range of sources of information.

## Vocabulary
household, role, responsibility

## Resources
Pens, paper and drawing materials; range of resource packs, books and internet resources on Ancient Greece, home and family life, for example: www.ancientgreece.co.uk/dailylife/home_set.html, www.woodlands-junior.kent.sch.uk/Homework/Greece.html and www.thehistorychannel.co.uk/site/microsites/ancientGreece/flash.php

## Links
NLS Y5 T1 Text 26: to make notes for different purposes.
NC Citizenship KS2: (1a) to explain their views, on issues that affect themselves and society.
NC English KS2: En1 (3) to talk effectively as members of a group.
NC ICT KS2: (1a) to talk about what information they need and how they can find and use it.

## Background
The lives of men and women in Ancient Greece differed considerably throughout the period. From childhood, boys were trained in martial arts and sports, with the aim of preparing them for warfare. Girls were brought up at home by their mothers and were taught the skills of the housewife. Women did not take part in public life and tended to be confined to upstairs rooms in their homes even when their husbands were entertaining their guests. Homes would usually contain three generations, with the grandparents living there too. A man would automatically be the head of the household, regardless of his age. Care may be needed if there are children from different cultural backgrounds in the class, perhaps where the role of women in society is still a current issue.

## Introduction
● Talk about how homes are run today and the sorts of jobs different people do in a household.
● Explain how home life in ancient times was similar in many ways to today, but there were some differences.
● Prompt the children to consider these differences and find out what they already know with questions such as: *What were the roles of men, women and children in Ancient Greece?*

## Main teaching activity
● Divide the class into boys and girls. Explain that the boys are going to find out what boys in Ancient Greece had to do and what their fathers worked at. The girls will investigate the roles of women and girls.
● Provide the children with a wide range of different resources, such as resource packs, books or internet sites to research this topic themselves.
● Organise boys and girls to work in small groups and to focus on specific aspects of their research theme, for example: girls' dress, work in the home, and so on.
● Ask the groups to assemble a page of information in the form of notes, sketches and pictures about their topic for use later in the class guidebook.

## Plenary
● Bring the class together to share their findings and to debate their views on these different roles. Encourage them to consider why the lives of boys and girls, women and men, were so different at this time in history. Would they like to have lived in the time of Ancient Greece?

## Differentiation
Provide adult support as necessary in the research activities.

# Who was Pythagoras?

## Objectives
● To find out about the events, people and changes studied from an appropriate range of sources of information.

## Vocabulary
Pythagoras, theorem, philosopher

## Resources
Range of resource packs, books and internet resources about Pythagoras and Greek scholars in general, for example: www.ancientgreece.co.uk/ knowledge/home_set.html and www.woodlands-junior. kent.sch.uk/Homework/ greece/famous.htm; the photocopiable sheet 'Account of Pythagoras and his school' on page 116, one per child; pens and paper.

## Links
NLS Y5 T1 Text 26: to make notes for different purposes.
NC Citizenship KS2: (4b) to think about the lives of people living in other places and times, and people with different values and customs.
NC ICT KS2: (1a) to talk about what information they need and how they can find and use it.

## Background
Pythagoras is still very relevant to teaching and learning in mathematics in the present day. His theory is still used in schools to teach about the lengths of the sides of a right-angled triangle. He lived between 580 and 500BC and, although his major interest was in mathematics, as was a common interest in Ancient Greece, he was known as a philosopher. He taught the theory of reincarnation and many new ideas related to astronomy. Pythagoras' 'school', however, was less of what we would imagine, and more like a secret society, which lived very much by its own rules.

## Introduction
● Explain the lesson objectives to the class and ascertain their prior knowledge about the subject with questions such as: *Who was Pythagoras? What did he achieve?*

## Main teaching activity
● Study sources and accounts about schools in Ancient Greece and about the Greek scholar, Pythagoras.
● Discuss the things he was famous for, especially his theorem.
● Ask the children to explain how Greek mathematics and the work of Pythagoras continue in modern schools and find out exactly what Pythagoras' theory is.
● Give out the photocopiable sheet 'Account of Pythagoras and his school' on page 116 for the children to read. Make sure that the children understand the text, explaining any unfamiliar words to them.
● Ask the children to create a 'similarities and differences' chart, noting the differences between the type of school set up by Pythagoras and what we think of as a school today.
● Set the task for the children of finding out as much as possible about other famous scholars, such as Plato, Homer, Archimedes and Hippocrates.

## Plenary
● Encourage the class to think about how the work of Ancient Greek scholars is used today, for example: Hippocrates or Archimedes.

## Differentiation
Provide adult support as necessary in the chart-making activity. For less able children, it may be helpful to provide starter sentences as a framework for the chart of similarities and differences. More able children can be encouraged to research more about famous Greek scholars.

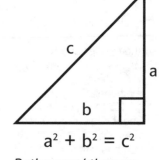

$$a^2 + b^2 = c^2$$

*Pythagoras' theorem*

# The Battle of Marathon

## Objectives
● To know about characteristic features of the period and societies studied.
● To recognise that the past is represented and interpreted in different ways, and to give reasons for this.
● To find out about the events, people and changes studied from visual sources and accounts.

## Vocabulary
armour, weapons, hoplite, Marathon

## Resources
Pictures of Greek soldiers and battles taken from books, resource packs and the internet; the photocopiable sheet 'The Battle of Marathon' on page 117, one per child.

## Links
NLS Y4 T3 Text 23: to present a point of view in writing.
NC English KS2: En3 (1d) to use and adapt the features of a form of writing, drawing on their reading.

## Background
One of the best sources of pictures showing Greeks at war is pottery. There are many written sources too, and we know about the events that happened at the battle of Marathon from the writings of Herodotus, an Ancient Greek historian.

Many images of warfare have been preserved on the sides of vases, reflecting the importance of warfare in the lives of the Ancient Greeks. Greek warriors, or 'hoplites', wore metal crested helmets. They carried a shield, called a 'hoplon', a spear and short sword in battle and they would often wear body armour made of bronze or linen reinforced with metal. The amount and quality of armour that a soldier wore depended on how well he or his family could afford to equip him.

Hoplites often fought in a battle formation called a 'phalanx'. A phalanx was made up of about 10,000 soldiers arranged into groups. In each group, or unit, there were 16 (or 8) rows with 16 (or 8) men in each row. The hoplites in the front rows held very long spears in front of them to push through the enemy. The hoplites in the back rows held their spears upright, ready to move forward as the men in front fell down dead or wounded.

## Introduction
● Explain the lesson objectives to the class - that is: the past is often interpreted in different ways.
● Discuss and explore the notion of 'bias' and the meaning of 'unbiased', giving examples that the children can easily relate to.

## Main teaching activity
● Look at pictures of Greek soldiers and battles to provide a context for the lesson.
● Provide the class with copies of the photocopiable sheet 'The Battle of Marathon' on page 117, which is written from a Greek point of view.
● When the children have read and thought about the account, ask them to identify and list the points which they feel might seem biased if they were a Persian reading it.
● Set the children the task of writing another account, as if written by a Persian, which they can compose from the information in the account they have read.

## Plenary
● Bring the class together in a discussion of sources and the importance of being aware of bias in accounts, not only in history but also in the present day, such as in newspapers.

## Differentiation
Provide adult support as necessary in the written activity.

# The first Olympic Games

## Objectives
● To know about characteristic features of the period and societies studied.
● To find out about the events, people and changes studied from visual sources and accounts.

## Vocabulary
Olympia, Olympic, stadium

## Resources
The completed photocopiable sheet 'Map of Ancient Greece' on page 115 or another similar map; pens, paper and drawing materials; variety of written and visual sources on the Ancient Greek Games, including images on Greek pottery, for example, using websites such as www.ancient-greece.co.uk/festivals/story/olympics.html and www.thebritishmuseum.ac.uk/compass/ (see under 'Tours').

## Links
NLS Y5 T1 Text 26: to make notes for different purposes.
NC English KS2 En1 (3) to talk effectively as members of a group.
NC Geography KS2: (2c) to use atlases and globes, and maps and plans at a range of scales.

## Background

The first Olympic Games took place in 776BC at Olympia. The games lasted for several days and were held every four years. There was an area containing religious buildings and temples, the most important being the Temple of Zeus, in which stood a huge gold and ivory statue of Zeus, over 12 metres high. Outside this area were the priests' houses, baths, guesthouses and accommodation for the athletes. On one side of the stadium there was a stone platform on which the judges sat and there was room for 45,000 spectators, all men.

Both short- and long-distance races were run at the ancient Olympic Games, along with wrestling, boxing, jumping, javelin, discus, horse riding and chariot racing. The Ancient Greeks took their sports very seriously and physical fitness was considered essential for all young men, so that they would be ready for war, should it be necessary. In fact, the word 'athlete' is derived from the Greek. It is thought by some that the games originated as part of the preparation of young men for warfare. Branches of the olive tree that grew next to the Temple of Zeus were used to make wreaths, which were placed on the heads of winning athletes.

## Introduction

● Explain the lesson objectives and ask the class what they already know about the history of the Olympic Games.
● Discuss where they began, the origins of the name and why the children think the games were held.

## Main teaching activity

● Look at a map of Ancient Greece (perhaps using the photocopiable sheet 'Map of Ancient Greece' on page 115, completed by the children in Lesson 2), and identify the site at Olympia of the ancient games.
● Provide the class with a variety of sources – visual and written.
● Divide the class into groups and set each group a different topic to work on, for example: short- and long-distance races, wrestling, boxing, jumping, javelin, discus, horse riding and chariot racing.
● Ask each group to produce a page of information for the class guidebook about their specific Olympic sport, including an illustration of the event in the style of Greek artwork on pottery. These can then be added to the guidebook along with modern-day images of athletes and the Olympics.

## Plenary

● Display the pages produced and discuss the new information they contain, such as why the games originated and why they still continue.

## Differentiation

Working in mixed ability groups will provide support for the less able.

# The theatre in Ancient Greece

## Objectives
● To know about characteristic features of the period and societies studied.
● To find out about the events, people and changes studied from visual sources and written sources.

## Vocabulary
tragedy, comedy, drama, chorus

## Resources
Video material, pictures and resources showing Greek drama, scenes and the chorus (for example, the website www.bbc.co.uk/schools/ancient greece); the photocopiable sheet 'Masks for the theatre' on page 118, one per child; art materials.

## Links
NC Art and design KS2: (1a) to record from experience and imagination, to select and record from first-hand observation and to explore ideas for different purposes
NC English KS2: En1 (4a) to create, adapt and sustain different roles, individually and in groups.

## Background
Singing and dancing were as much a part of Greek culture in ancient times as they are today. Greek theatre grew out of the festival held in honour of Dionysus, the god of wine. The theatres were large, semi-circular constructions built on hillsides. They were open air and could seat over 18,000 spectators. Seating was tiered around the semi-circle in the auditorium and the seats were stone steps, giving a good view of the circular floor of the theatre, known as the orchestra. The 'skene' was a raised hut in which the actors, all men, could change. A greek playwright had the idea to paint the skene, creating scenery. The actors wore large masks designed to show particular emotions, such as sadness or anger. Plays were either tragedies, often set in the past, or comedies about everyday life.

## Introduction
● Talk about the theatre in Ancient Greece and ask the class what they have heard about it already.
● Suggest that they now begin to think about the question: *What can we learn about Ancient Greek theatre and drama?*

## Main teaching activity
● Use video material and pictures to teach the class about the particular features and style of Greek drama, such as the use of a chorus and the wearing of masks.
● Ask the children to choose a character from modern times.
● Give each child a copy of photocopiable sheet 'Masks for the theatre' on page 118. This worksheet can be used for reference but may also be enlarged for use as a mask template.
● Provide materials for the children to make masks in the Greek style, with exaggerated expressions. The masks need to typify the type of character they have chosen.
● If there is time, challenge the children, working in small groups, to act out scenes from the life of their chosen character wearing their masks.

## Plenary
● Display the masks or ask groups of children to perform their short scenes in front of the rest of the class.

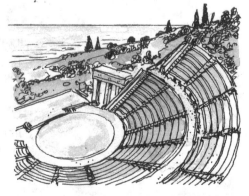

## Differentiation
Provide adult support for the children in the art activity.

# Heroes from Ancient Greece

● To find out about the events, people and changes studied from an appropriate range of sources of information.

## Vocabulary
Alexander the Great, Odysseus, Jason, Theseus, Perseus

## Resources
The photocopiable sheet 'The life of Alexander the Great' on page 119, one per child; information about the lives of heroes from ancient Greece or Greek mythology (useful websites include www.woodlands-junior. kent.sch.uk/Homework/ greece/famous.htm and www.discoverychannel. co.uk/greece

## Links
NLS Y4 T1 Text 13: to write playscripts; Y5 T1 Text 26: to make notes for different purposes.
NC English KS2: En3 (1d) to use and adapt the features of a form of writing, drawing on their reading.

## Background
Heroes and heroism were really important ideas in Ancient Greece. Heroes were venerated in both Greek histories and in their mythology. This lesson provides an opportunity for children to think carefully about a concept and to make meaningful links between the past and the present.

## Introduction
● Ask the class if they know of any Greek heroes.
● Explain that in this lesson, they are going to find out more about Greek heroes and think about how to display what they have learned and discovered.

## Main teaching activity
● Talk about the notion of a hero and how the word originates from Greek.
● Invite the children to think of some modern-day heroes and discuss the qualities that make someone a hero.
● Read together the photocopiable sheet 'The life of Alexander the Great' on page 119. Make sure that the children understand the passage and discuss together what they think makes Alexander the Great a hero.
● Ask the children to choose another hero from Ancient Greek history, for example: Odysseus, Jason, Hercules, Theseus or Perseus.
● Ensure the children have enough information about their chosen hero's life, or access to suitable internet sites, to enable them to research information and to make up some scenes about key events.
● Challenge the children to write a short dramatic episode featuring their hero, written as a playscript. For example, they might choose to act out a scene from the Odyssey.

## Plenary
● Organise a reading of the playscripts in small groups.

## Differentiation
Provide adult support as necessary in the research and written activities.

# How ideas from Ancient Greece have influenced us

### Objectives
● To recall, select and organise historical information.
● To communicate their knowledge and understanding of history in a variety of ways.

### Vocabulary
concept, heritage, styles, influence

### Resources
Children's work and wall displays; pens, paper and drawing materials.

### Links
NLS Y5 T1 Text 26: to make notes for different purposes; Y6 T3 Text 21 to divide whole texts into paragraphs, paying attention to the sequence of paragraphs and to links between one paragraph and the next.
NC English KS2: En1 (3) to talk effectively as members of a group.
NC PSHE & citizenship KS2: (2g) to know what democracy is and about the basic institutions that support it locally and nationally.

## Background
This lesson encourages the children to make direct links between their knowledge of history and the present day. The activities suggested encourage them to think carefully about their previous learning and to analyse it in a new way – that is: the ideas that lay behind much of what the Ancient Greeks created.

## Introduction
● Explain that in this lesson the class are going to work on the following question: *How have ideas from Ancient Greece influenced us today?*
● Discuss the wide range of concepts that can be considered as 'ideas'.
● Talk about whether it is only concepts such as democracy that the Greeks have left behind.

## Main teaching activity
● Ask the class to think of as many different examples drawn from an Ancient Greek heritage as they can, for example: language, sports and the Olympic Games, gods and mythology, theatre, schools, scholars, medicine, buildings, and ideas such as democracy.
● Look back at the children's work and wall displays to help them recall the topics they have studied.
● Ask the children what they have discovered for themselves while at home or while using the internet or reading books.
● Choose a number of examples to discuss with the children to model ways of making comparisons.
● Provide a format for them to write to, perhaps using this example:
  First, explain the original example as it was in Ancient Greek times, using the idea of democracy as an example.
  Second, explain how this idea is still used today.
  Third, explain how the idea has changed and how it has stayed the same.
● Encourage the children to write in paragraphs, one for each of the sections that are suggested for their writing.
● Set them the task of creating a piece of extended writing about their chosen aspect and also of creating an illustration, both of which can be included in the class book.

## Plenary
● Ask individuals to explain their particular example and why they chose it. Discuss what idea or concept lay behind it.

## Differentiation
Provide adult support as necessary in the written activities.

# A guidebook about Ancient Greece

## Objectives
● To recall, select and organise historical information.
● To communicate their knowledge and understanding of history in a variety of ways.

## Vocabulary
all the vocabulary from the topic

## Resources
Materials for book making; access to computers for word-processing.

## Background
This activity provides a good opportunity for a variety of assessment strategies to be used. Direct observation during the discussion and making processes will enable the teacher to note those children with a good grasp of the key historical skills and concepts. Listening to children's conversations can be revealing of their level of knowledge and awareness of time, change causation and so on. Marking can also be carried out once the book has been completed, as a final summative piece of assessment.

## Introduction
● Explain to the class that they are now at the stage of completing their guidebook. They need to think carefully about what will be useful to include and how to present it.
● They will need to consider the following question: What is important to tell visitors about Ancient Greece?

## Main teaching activity
● Organise the class to work in small groups or pairs.
● Encourage the children to discuss the contents and presentation of their chapters and then provide time for the work to be completed.
● Ask the children to consider how the chapters should be arranged – is there a particular order which would make most sense to a reader? What should come first? What should come last?
● Invite the children to create a suitable cover, if there is time, and, finally, assemble all the work into a guidebook.

## Plenary
● Ask children to summarise and present their work to the class, to visitors or another class in the school. Marking or reviewing of the finished book can also be used as an assessment opportunity.

## Differentiation
Organise the class to work in mixed ability pairs or groups to provide support for the less able children.

## Links
NLS Y5 T1 Text 26: to make notes for different purposes.
NLS Y3 T1 Text 23: to write simple non-chronological reports from known information. Write for a known audience; Y3 T3 Text 21: to use IT to bring work to a published form – discuss relevance of layout, font, and so on; Y4 T3 Text 24: to summarise in writing the key ideas. NC English KS2: En3 (1d) to use and adapt the features of a form of writing, drawing on their reading.

# Map of Ancient Greece

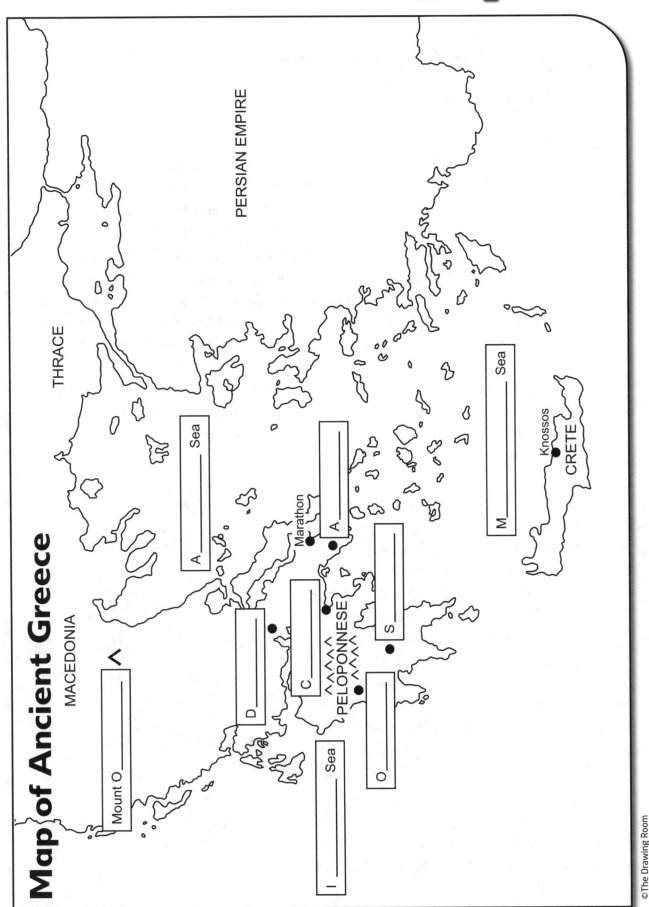

MACEDONIA

THRACE

PERSIAN EMPIRE

Mount O _____

A _____ Sea

A _____ Sea

Marathon

D _____

C _____

PELOPONNESE

S _____

O _____

_____ Sea

M _____ Sea

Knossos

CRETE

©The Drawing Room

# Account of Pythagoras and his school

Pythagoras, who lived between about 580 and 500BC, was probably born on the Greek island of Samos. When he grew up, he despised the government of his homeland, which he thought was tyrannical. Therefore, he left Greece and went to live in southern Italy in a town called Croton.

Pythagoras had always had a deep interest in mathematics and this led him to set up a school in Croton. The school was organised like a society where men and women interested in mathematics, religion, astronomy, philosophy and science could go to study and discuss their ideas. His group of scholars called themselves the Mathememtikoi, and became a sort of secret society. They lived according to a very strict code, eating together at set times, exercising, listening to religious teaching and studying. They sang hymns to Apollo, played musical instruments such as the lyre and held poetry recitations.

The school made important discoveries and innovations in the field of mathematics. Pythagoras and some of his students and colleagues believed that everything could be related to mathematics. They agreed that 'all is number'. Pythagoras is also famous for his theories about sound, but he is especially remembered for his work on the right-angled triangle. His theory is still used in schools today to teach about the lengths of the sides of a right-angled triangle.

Sadly no books by Pythagoras are known to exist and he is thought to have taught by word of mouth. However, he is mentioned in the works of other Greek writers such as Ovid. Pythagoras' school soon began to arouse suspicion and mistrust in Croton. Eventually, there were struggles amongst his followers, and suspicion of the school became so great that Pythagoras had to flee from Croton to Metapontum, where he is thought to have died.

# The Battle of Marathon

**M**any Greeks went to live in other nearby countries, which were part of the Ancient Greek Empire. However, in 499BC the Greeks living in one part of Persia decided to rebel against their cruel Persian rulers, who were becoming too strict and wicked in the way they treated the people. The Persian ruler Darius quashed this rebellion but was so angry that he wanted vengeance. So in 490BC, he decided to attack the mainland of Greece and then to attack Athens itself. He sent a huge army and 600 ships to attack the Greek mainland. They landed at the bay of Marathon.

The poor Athenians were taken totally by surprise. However, Militades, a clever Greek general, was used to the cunning tactics used by the Persians in warfare. He decided it was best to challenge them bravely rather than wait for them to attack first. He decided to send Pheidippides, a good athlete, to run to Sparta to ask for help. The Spartans were an important state within Greece and quite rightly should have helped Athens in this battle against the evil foreigners. Pheidippides ran almost continuously for two days and nights and when he reached Sparta he found that the Spartans were having a religious festival and they refused to help until the next full moon! By the time Pheidippides had run back to Marathon with the news, he had run over a hundred miles. He also had to fight in the battle. However, being a strong, well-trained Greek, he did this with no trouble.

The Greeks, using their usual clever tactics under their commander Militades, were able to defeat the huge Persian force, losing only 192 men themselves, while the Persians lost many more. Pheidippides survived the battle in spite of being exhausted after his long run. He was then ordered to take the news of the victory back to Athens. He once again ran all the way, told his good news and then, having done his duty, fell down dead. He is remembered as a great Greek hero to this day, partly through the marathon race in each modern Olympic Games, where athletes cover the same distance that he had to run all those years ago.

# Masks for the theatre

# The life of Alexander the Great

Alexander became king of Macedonia at the age of 20, after the murder of his father, Philip II. To begin with, Alexander had to spend time settling affairs in Greece and Macedonia. He marched into Greece and terrified the cities that were thinking of revolt and giving votes of thanks to his father's murderers. The Persians had paid the people of Thebes to rise against the Macedonian garrison there, so Alexander captured Thebes and destroyed it, leaving only one house standing. After only 15 months, the Greeks and countries neighbouring Macedonia had learned that this new, youthful ruler was a serious force to reckon with, and had learned their lesson.

Alexander's father had planned to invade the vast Persian Empire to the east of Greece and it was to this plan that Alexander turned to next. Over the next 11 years, 334–323BC, Alexander's army fought its way to India – defeating the Persian armies and taking over the whole of the huge Persian Empire, which included Egypt, Palestine, Iraq and Syria. Alexander won an empire for Greece that was the greatest the world had ever known. As King of Persia, and when dealing with Persian subjects, Alexander adopted Persian styles. This led to some resentment amongst his Greek officers, so he then dressed in Greek styles when dealing with Greeks.

Wherever he went, Alexander built new cities, calling many of them 'Alexandria' after himself. Consequently, there are many cities called by this name even today, like Alexandria in Egypt. His nickname 'megas' meant 'the great'. After many great adventures, including campaigns in Iran and Afghanistan, and while preparing a new campaign in Arabia, Alexander died, aged 32. Alexander was not a commonplace ruler; he was one of the most astonishing men in history. When Alexander died, the Greek Empire stretched from the Adriatic to the Indus, and from the Caspian to Upper Egypt.

# CHAPTER 7

# The Aztecs

Much of Aztec society is based on foundations laid by the earlier classic Mayan civilisation. However, far from being 'ancient', as is a common misconception, the Aztecs were a much later civilisation, contemporary with the early Tudor period in England.

At the time of the Spanish Conquest of the Aztecs, the Spanish found a society completely alien to them. In particular, they were shocked by the Aztec religious ceremonies that often involved human sacrifice. However, there were other aspects to Aztec culture. They accumulated a vast collection of books on history, astronomy and natural history, and pieces of Aztec sculpture and architecture from this period demonstrate their artistic accomplishment.

|  | OBJECTIVES | MAIN ACTIVITY |
|---|---|---|
| **Lesson 1** | To know about social, cultural, religious and ethnic diversity.<br>To recall, communicate and organise historical information. | A grid is used to establish what the children already know and want to find out about the Aztecs. |
| **Lesson 2** | To know about social, cultural, religious and ethnic diversity.<br>To find out about the past from a variety of sources. | Children identify, draw and label foods from Mexico. |
| **Lesson 3** ⓟ | To find out about the past from a variety of sources. | Children investigate the routes Spanish explorers took to reach the Aztecs. |
| **Lesson 4** ⓟ | To place events, people and changes into correct periods of time.<br>To use dates and vocabulary relating to the passing of time. | Children work on a large class timeline and then individual timelines. |
| **Lesson 5** | To find out about the past from artefacts.<br>To communicate their knowledge in a variety of ways. | Children investigate artefacts and describe an artefact for a partner to draw. |
| **Lesson 6** ⓟ | To find out about the past from historic sites.<br>To ask and answer questions, and to select and record information.<br>To communicate their knowledge in a variety of ways. | The Aztec capital city is researched as a class activity and children label a picture individually. |
| **Lesson 7** ⓟ | To find out about the past from stories and myths.<br>To ask and answer questions, and to select and record information.<br>To communicate their knowledge in a variety of ways. | Children read the Aztec creation myth and consider the likelihood of its truth compared to other theories. |
| **Lesson 8** ⓟ | To find out about the past from pictures and drawings. | Using pictures, children look at how the Aztecs dressed and the different types of work they did. |
| **Lesson 9** | To find out about the past from a variety of sources. | In groups, children consider different sources and what can be learned from them. |
| **Lesson 10** | To communicate their knowledge in a variety of ways. | Children perform dramatic scenes, using costumes and props they have made. |
| **Lesson 11** ⓟ | To find out about the past from poetry. | Children read an example of Aztec poetry and create a short dramatic scene showing the defeat of the Aztecs. |
| **Lesson 12** ⓟ | To recognise that the past is represented and interpreted in different ways. | Two accounts of the Aztecs' defeat show the children how historical accounts differ. |
| **Lesson 13** | To find out about the past from historic sites. | Children investigate pyramids and make their own models. |
| **Lesson 14** | To recall, select and organise historical information.<br>To use dates and historical vocabulary.<br>To communicate their knowledge in a variety of ways. | The children complete their grids from Lesson 1. |

# What do we know about the Aztecs

## Objectives
● To know about the social, cultural, religious and ethnic diversity of the societies studied, in Britain and the wider world.
● To recall, communicate and organise historical information.

## Vocabulary
Mexico, Mexica, America

## Resources
Grids with three columns, one per child (see illustration below); topic books on the Aztecs; globe or map of the world.

## Background
Many children will already have heard about the Aztecs, even if only from chocolate bars! But, in some cases, individuals may know a surprising amount. It can be very useful, as an initial activity, to find out how much children already know. This can help inform the choice of themes and activities subsequently. There is so much written and so many good sources about life in Aztec Mexico that even those children who may have already learned a significant amount will find much more to interest them.

Some aspects of this topic will seem unsavoury and even quite shocking. However, if treated carefully, and as part of the whole of the Aztecs' belief system, their religious practices and sacrificial rites can be taught sympathetically. To the modern world, the ritual practice of human sacrifice seems very barbaric, but it is important to remember that this is a practice that has occurred in most parts of the world at some point in history, and is not specific to the history of Mexico.

## Introduction
● Explain that in this lesson the children will be remembering what they have heard about a group of people in the past called the Aztecs. Tell them that another name for them is 'Mexica'.
● Prompt the class to recall what they already know about the Aztecs with questions such as: *Where did they live? Where is this on a globe? What were they like?*

| What I already know | What I want to know | What I have learned |
|---|---|---|
|  |  |  |
|  |  |  |
|  |  |  |
|  |  |  |
|  |  |  |
|  |  |  |
|  |  |  |

## Main teaching activity
● Give the children each a copy of the grid.
● Ask them to put in the first column what they know at present, in the second column what they want to know, and to leave the third column blank so that they can add what they have learned later on.
● This part of the lesson could be carried out as a shared writing activity.

## Plenary
● Provide the children with topic books for their work on the Aztecs and give them time to paste their grid into the back of their book.

## Links
NLS Y4 T2 Text 23: to collect information from a variety of sources and present it in one simple format.

## Differentiation
Provide additional adult support as necessary for the less able writers in the writing activity. Encourage more able children to work independently and to think carefully about the sorts of information they would like to find out.

# Aztec food

## Background
Food in modern Mexico is, in some ways, very similar to the food of the Aztecs. Mexicans from a native Indian heritage eat tortillas, made from maize, beans, chillies and both red and green tomatoes. In fact many of these foods are typical of Mexico and have also become available internationally. Chocolate, in particular, is a well-known food, although the Aztecs tended to drink it rather than eat it as confectionery. A famous savoury Mexican dish is 'mole poblano', made with chicken or turkey in a spicy chocolate sauce; it is very hot and full of chillies! This suggests, perhaps, that the Aztecs too might have used chocolate as a spice for cooking. Another unusual food for the Aztecs was the small dog, the Chihuahua. They ate only birds, fish and small animals, since there were no large animals, such as cows or sheep, until they were brought into the region by Europeans. If the children are going to taste any of the foods, make sure you check for allergies and dietary requirements first.

## Introduction
● Ask: *What did the Aztecs eat?* Ask the children what sort of things they think the Aztecs might have eaten. Would their food have been the same as ours?
● Explain that some of the things they ate were very different from what we are used to, and seem a little strange to us, but tell the class that we actually eat many things that originated with the Aztecs today in Britain.

## Main teaching activity
● Set out a selection of foods from Mexixo for the children to see, such as chillies, chocolate, tomatoes and maize.
● Ask the children to identify them and then ask if they know where they first came from.
● Discuss how they were first grown and eaten by the Aztecs and then how they were introduced into Europe by the Spanish following the conquest of the Aztecs.
● Taste, draw and label some of the items, but be very careful with the chillies. It is important not to chew raw chilli or get it in your eyes.

## Plenary
● Make a display of the children's pictures to start off a wall display about the Aztecs. Discuss what other foods the children know of that originated in other parts of the world, for example: currry, ingredients for Chinese food, such as bamboo shoots, water chestnuts and so on.

## Differentiation
Direct questions according to ability. Provide additional support in the drawing and labelling tasks for children with special needs.

# Locating the Aztecs

## Objectives
● To find out about the events, people and changes studied from an appropriate range of sources of information.

## Vocabulary
voyages, routes, terrain, mountainous, jungle, desert

## Resources
Globe of the world; pictures of native Americans from Central America, especially Aztecs, and pictures of the landscape from books such as *Aztec, Inca and Maya* by Elizabeth Baquedano (DK publishing) and *Step into the Aztec and Maya World* by Fiona Macdonald (Lorenz Books) and websites including www.mexicolore.co.uk/; the photocopiable sheet 'How the Spanish explorers found the Aztecs' on page 135, one per child and one enlarged.

## Links
NC Geography KS2: (1a) to ask geographical questions; (2a) to use appropriate geographical vocabulary; (2c) to use atlases and globes, and maps and plans at a range of scales.
NC PSHE & citizenship KS2: (4b) to think about the lives of people living in other places and times, and people with different values and customs.

## Background
A study of a past society such as the Aztecs requires an understanding of the geographical context as well as the historical. Mexico is very remote from Britain and Europe both in terms of its location and also the type of terrain found there. High mountain ranges, vast jungles and huge deserts make Mexico a very diversified country. This terrain, and the fact that travel and communications have always been difficult until very recent times, means that many different social groups, with different customs and languages, were a feature of this part of the world. The central region of Mexico, where Mexico City now stands, was the site of the Aztec capital, Tenochtitlan. Children will need to appreciate the size, diversity and great difference in the location of the Aztecs compared with the UK.

## Introduction
● Initiate discussion about Mexico's location with questions such as: *Where did the Aztecs live? What was their country like?*

## Main teaching activity
● Use a large globe of the world to locate Mexico and compare its size in relation to Britain.
● Explain how Columbus and then Cortés sailed around the world to discover the Americas first, tracing their routes there on the globe.
● Look together at the enlarged version of the photocopiable sheet 'How the Spanish explorers found the Aztecs' on page 135. Discuss the routes that the Spanish explorers took. Talk about how the winds and tides helped them to sail there (and back to Spain) quite easily.
● Show and discuss a selection of pictures showing the landscapes.
● Consider pictures of the people who lived there, such as the Aztecs, noting differences in their appearance compared with people from Europe, for example: skin colour, facial appearance, dress, and so on.
● Provide the children with a copy each of the photocopiable sheet on page 135 to trace the routes the explorers and 'conquistadors' took.

## Plenary
● Discuss the differences and similarities between the Central American peoples and those from other parts of the world. Talk about the diversity of peoples even within the continent of America. Explain that the Native North Americans were quite different, for example, in their dress, their customs and lives (they were hunters and nomadic, while the Aztecs were town and city dwellers). Explain that these were the people the Spanish explorers found after their journeys across the Atlantic.

## Differentiation
Provide support with mapwork tasks for children with special needs.

# Aztec timeline

## Objectives
● To place events, people and changes into correct periods of time.
● To use dates and vocabulary relating to the passing of time.

## Vocabulary
Empire, emperor, invade, conquer

## Resources
Large class timeline, divided into centuries from AD300 to AD1600 for the wall; three cards containing a few dates and words about the following events: the setting up of the Aztec capital city; the discovery of the Aztecs by Cortés; the conquest of the Aztecs by the Spanish; the photocopiable sheet 'Aztec timeline' on page 136, one per child and one set of cards enlarged.

## Links
NNS Y3-4: number sequences, place value and ordering.

## Background
The Aztecs, although sometimes described as an 'ancient' civilisation, were contemporary with the early Tudor period in England. It is possible that they have been considered ancient because of the different stage of technological development that was evident when the first Europeans arrived there. While they knew about the wheel, they did not make the same uses of it as in Europe, such as for transport. They tended to make much use of stone for tools and weapons, which is sometimes seen as a feature of a less well-developed society. However, in other ways, the Aztecs were beginning to develop rapidly at the time of the Spanish Conquest. They are thought to have first founded Tenochtitlan, their capital city, in 1325. The causeways to the mainland were built and the Emperor Itzacoatl invaded and took over surrounding lands in 1427. In 1440 Moctezuma I first began to spread Aztec rule throughout the region. By 1489 the Aztecs were beginning to penetrate Mayan areas in the south. In 1502 Moctezuma II was crowned, only to see his empire invaded in 1519 and conquered by 1521. The last Aztec Emperor, Cuauhtémoc, was killed in 1525.

## Introduction
● Ask the class if anyone knows when the Aztecs lived, and when they ruled in Mexico.
● Ask: *When did people from outside Mexico find out about them?*

## Main teaching activity
● Discuss the cards with the class and ask for volunteers to place them on the large timeline on the wall.
● Think about how long the Aztecs ruled before they were invaded. Explain how they had taken over most of Central Mexico and turned it into their own empire.
● Discuss the meaning of 'empire' and compare it with the British Empire of the 19th and 20th centuries.
● Give out copies of the photocopiable sheet 'Aztec timeline' on page 136 and let the children complete them. They will need to arrange the information labels in the correct places on their timelines. Concepts of time and an understanding of chronology, sequencing, dates and the words associated with these skills can be checked during this task.

## Plenary
● Review sequencing of events and dates together, and ask children to place enlarged versions of the cards on the class timeline.

## Differentiation
Provide additional adult support during the timeline activities as required.

# Aztec artefacts

## Objectives
● To find out about the events, people and changes studied from artefacts.
● To communicate their knowledge and understanding of history in a variety of ways.

## Vocabulary
object, artefact, replica

## Resources
Range of artefacts or replica artefacts from Mexico, or instead, a variety of pictures of these (for example, websites such as www.thebritishmuseum.ac.uk/compass (see under 'Tours'), www.newodysseyart.co.uk and www.mexicolore.co.uk/); sketching materials.

## Links
NC English KS2: En1 (3) to talk effectively as members of a group.
NC Art and design KS2: (1a) to record from experience and imagination, to select and record from first-hand observation and to explore ideas for different purposes.

## Background
Objects from the past can form a vital part of children's understanding of a past society. They are especially useful if explained within a meaningful context, so that the child is more able to relate to them and understand the reasons for them appearing different from things they are used to in Britain. In addition to learning new information and knowledge about the period studied, the use of artefacts as 'clues' about the past can also help develop children's skills in asking historical questions. It can promote their ability to think, to make inferences and deductions, as well as encouraging them to rely on their own interpretations and to be critical of the sources they use. All these skills and qualities will be useful for their future intellectual development.

## Introduction
● Provide a variety of artefacts, replica artefacts or photographs of artefacts for the children to discuss.
● Allow time for the children to look at, handle and talk about them.
● Explain that in this lesson the class is going to find out more about the Aztecs from looking at some of the things they made.

## Main teaching activity
● Lead the children's investigation with a number of open questions, such as: *What are the objects made from? Why did the Aztecs make them? What were they for? Who might have used them?* It might be useful here to work as a whole class, especially if the children have little prior experience of working with artefacts. If they already have these skills, then you might prefer to organise the class to work in groups with a selection of artefacts for each group.
● Next, organise the class to work in pairs. There needs to be a screen or divider between the children, so that one child can conceal an object from the other.
● Give one child in each pair an artefact (or picture of an artefact), hidden from their partner.
● Ask the child to describe the artefact without showing it to their partner.
● The second child then draws a picture of the object from the description given.

## Plenary
● Allow time for the children to share the pictures with each other and to see how accurate their descriptions were. Share some particularly good ones with the whole class.

## Differentiation
Direct questions at appropriate levels of difficulty.

# Pictures of Tenochtitlan

## Objectives
● To find out about the events, people and changes studied from historic sites.
● To ask and answer questions, and to select and record information relevant to the focus of the enquiry.
● To communicate their knowledge and understanding of history in a variety of ways.

## Vocabulary
Tenochtitlan, swamp

## Resources
Pictures and plans of the Aztec capital city of Tenochtitlan, for example from websites such as: http://www.azteca.net/aztec/prehisp/teotihua.html, www.newodyssey art.co.uk/ancient_mexico_photo_tour.html and www.mexicocity.com.mx/teoti_i.html; the photocopiable sheet 'An artist's idea of what Tenochtitlan looked like' on page 137, one per child; description of Tenochtitlan by Bernal Diaz from http://www.pbs.org/opb/conquistadors/mexico/adventure1/pop-tenochtitlan.htm; whiteboard or OHP.

## Links
NLS Y3 T2 Text 17: to make clear notes.
NC English KS2: En1 (3) to talk effectively as members of a group.

## Background
The first pictorial map of Tenochtitlan was drawn by the Spanish commander Cortés, no doubt to help him with his invasion plans. The map is quite detailed and shows the civic and religious buildings as well as the numerous streets, canals and houses. One of Cortés' soldiers, Bernal Diaz, was overwhelmed at the sight of the city when he first saw it from the mountains above. He thought it was the most beautiful place he had ever set eyes upon. It was filled with waterways, trees and immaculately clean streets. From the map and the descriptions we have, models and reconstructions have been made and artists have been able to draw what we think the city probably looked like.

## Introduction
● Explain to the class that this lesson is about the famous Aztec city.
● Ask if anyone has heard of it before and tell the children its name.
● Prompt the children with questions, such as: *Where can the remains be seen? What city is there now?*
● Explain that the site of Tenochtitlan is now Mexico City, one of the largest cities in the world.

## Main teaching activity
● Show the class pictures and plans of Tenochtitlan on the whiteboard or overhead projector.
● Explain to them how grand this city was when the Spaniards first saw it, and how many people lived there. The city is thought to have contained about half a million people, and to have been clean, well organised and full of beautiful plants and trees.
● Point out the large civic buildings in the centre, along with the Great Temple and the other large central temples.
● Ask the children what else they think was there, what kind of city this might have been, how important it was to the Aztecs and whether it was a special city. Make notes on the whiteboard.
● Give out copies of the photocopiable sheet 'An artist's idea of what Tenochtitlan looked like' on page 137 and encourage the children to annotate their picture, labelling it with the clues that show it was an important place for the Aztecs. They can use the notes previously made to help them with their writing task.

## Plenary
● Review the clues that the children have found, and conclude by reading the description of Tenochtitlan written by one of the first Europeans to see it, Bernal Diaz (see Resources).

## Differentiation
Provide additional adult support during the writing activities.

# The beginning of the Aztec Empire

## Objectives
- To find out about the events, people and changes studied from stories and myths.
- To ask and answer questions, and to select and record information relevant to the focus of the enquiry.
- To communicate their knowledge and understanding of history in a variety of ways.

## Vocabulary
creation myth, nomads, nomadic

## Resources
The photocopiable sheet 'How the Aztecs chose a place to settle' on page 138, one per child; two-column grid for the children to complete.

## Links
NLS Y3 T2 Text 17: to make clear notes; Y4 T2 Text 23: to collect information from a variety of sources and present it one simple format.
NC English KS2: En1 (3) to talk effectively as members of a group.

## Background
The real history of the Aztecs (or Mexica, as they were called) before they settled in the central valley of Mexico, is not known. It is thought that successive rulers rewrote their early history to show themselves in a good light, thus obscuring the real truth. Many historians believe, however, that the Aztecs probably started out as a small nomadic tribe, moving southwards from northern Mexico, and finally settling in Lake Texcoco. They were quite unpopular with other groups in the area, largely because of their religious rituals, which entailed capturing and sacrificing people from other tribes to their gods. They had many rites and rituals which were considered unpleasant by other tribes, not least the flaying alive of their victims and then dressing up in their skins!

This unpopularity may well have accounted for the fact that they frequently had to move on to new areas, and eventually the only place they could find to settle was an island in a snake-infested swampy area surrounded by a lake. Their own preferred account, however, gives a better version of why they settled there (see 'The Aztec creation myth' on the photocopiable sheet on page 138).

## Introduction
- Say to the class that the Aztecs settled in a most unusual area, and that they made up a story to tell others to explain why they had settled there.

## Main teaching activity
- Read together the story 'The Aztec creation myth' on the photocopiable sheet 'How the Aztecs chose a place to settle'.
- Prompt the children with questions such as: *Who told this story? Why did they tell it? What does it explain about Tenochtitlan?*
- Discuss whether the story really explains why the Aztecs chose to live in the middle of a lake.
- Read with the class the second passage 'Reasons why the Aztecs might have settled in Texcoco' from the photocopiable sheet and talk about it together.
- Give the children a grid with two headings: 'Reasons why the Aztecs chose to live here' and 'Reasons why they had to live here'.
- The class can work in pairs to complete their grids with short notes.

## Plenary
- Hold a vote to decide which version the class really believes.

## Differentiation
Working in mixed ability pairs will provide support for the less able.

# What do pictures of Aztecs tell us?

## Objectives
● How to find out about the events, people and changes studied from pictures and drawings.

## Vocabulary
hierarchy, headdress, loincloth

## Resources
The photocopiable sheet 'What the Aztecs looked like' on page 139; selection of illustrations from picture packs, internet sites or books, such as *The Broken Spears: The Aztec Account of the Conquest of Mexico* by Miguel Leon-Portilla (Beacon Press); writing and drawing materials.

## Links
NLS Y3 T2 Text 17: to make clear notes; Y4 T2 Text 23: to collect information from a variety of sources and present it one simple format. NC English KS2: En1 (3) to talk effectively as members of a group. NC Art and design KS2: (1a) to record from experience and imagination, to select and record from first-hand observation and to explore ideas for different purposes.

## Background
The Aztec social hierarchy and roles in society were clearly represented by the clothes worn by different people. The Aztecs wore linen robes, longer for more important men and shorter for ordinary men. Slaves wore loincloths. Women and girls wore long dresses. As with the amount of material, the colours used depended on the status of the wearer – the more important you were the more colourful your clothes. Feathers, shells and animal skins were widely used. For priests, masks and elaborate headdresses were common.

## Introduction
● Introduce the lesson with questions about what the Aztecs actually looked like and what they did, such as: *What do we know about the sort of clothes they wore? What sort of work did they do?*

## Main teaching activity
● Ask the children to make a collection of drawings and pictures of Aztec people, including some drawings made by the Aztecs themselves, for example, from *The Broken Spears* by Miguel Leon-Portilla.
● Discuss what the pictures show. Ask the children what they can say about the lives of Aztec men, women and children from looking at the drawings, for example – what sort of clothes they wore.
● Explain how there was a strict social hierarchy, which was reflected in the sort of clothes people at different levels were allowed to wear. In general, slaves wore very little, just a loincloth, while very rich people wore long, elaborate, highly-coloured clothes.
● Use further pictures showing the Aztecs at work to identify the sorts of jobs they did.
● Give the children a writing activity, differentiated for the different abilities in the class, to complete some sentences about their conclusions.

## Plenary
● Provide time for the children to illustrate their written descriptions.

## Differentiation
Provide sentence starters or a writing frame for the less able writers. For the very able writers this is an ideal opportunity for some extended, descriptive writing.

# Evaluating objects and texts from Aztec times

## Background

Children can learn a great deal from working with objects from the past, whether original or replicas. Objects from Aztec times will, of course, be replicas or pictures and photographs. Although little survives compared with what was found by the Spanish invaders, there is still a considerable amount of material that can be used. Things that have survived include some headdresses, a few books or codices, shields, knives made of obsidian (a dark, glassy volcanic rock), toys, pottery, many statues and figurines and architecture. The objects need to be explained within a meaningful context, however, so that the children are more able to relate to them and see their function. In addition to learning new information and knowledge about the period studied, the use of artefacts as 'clues' about the past can also help develop children's skills in asking historical questions. It can promote their ability to think, to make inferences and deductions, as well as encouraging them to be critical of the sources they use.

## Introduction

● Tell the children that they are going to try to answer questions such as: *What do the sources tell us about the Aztecs? Do some sources tell us more than others?*
● Explain that the most important question for the children is: *Which are the most useful sources?*

## Main teaching activity

● Provide a range of sources, such as: photographs of architecture, examples of Aztec art, codices, artefacts and Spanish texts.
● Organise the children to work in groups and provide each group with a different type of source.
● Invite the groups to think about the key things that they could say about the Aztecs from looking at their selection of sources.
● Ask the children to list what they can learn from their different sources. Then ask the children to evaluate their sources – which sources are the most useful?

## Plenary

● Complete a shared writing session to record each group's opinions and findings in the form of a simple chart. Finally hold a quick vote to find which type of source the children rate most highly.

## Differentiation

Organise the children to work in groups of similar abilities. Provide sources suitable for the abilities in each group, for example, visual sources for the less able and written sources for the more able.

# The Aztecs meet Cortés

### Objectives
● To communicate their knowledge and understanding of history in a variety of ways.

### Vocabulary
conqueror, invasion, conquest

### Resources
Materials for costumes and objects for the children to make (for example: fabrics, cardboard boxes, gold foil, feathers, tins, tubes and containers for home-made instruments).

### Links
NLS Y4 T1 Text 13: to write playscripts.
NC English KS2: En1 (4a) to create, adapt and sustain different roles, individually and in groups.
NC PSHE & citizenship KS2: (4b) to think about the lives of people living in other places and times, and people with different values and customs.

## Background
The meeting between Cortés and Moctezuma is perhaps among the most famous in history and it was certainly a momentous event at the time. It is a good theme for dramatic re-enactment. Moctezuma's messengers had seen the Spanish ships arriving, but had not been sure what they were, describing them as 'floating mountains'. The Indian tribes in the region where the Spanish first arrived sometimes welcomed them and sometimes fought them. However, Cortés, the Spanish commander, knew that the centre of power in the vast empire lay in the valley of Mexico. He found out all he could in advance and then led his army towards the Aztec capital.

Moctezuma, meanwhile, had been suffering greatly from an inability to act. He was at first convinced that these white people were gods, returned from their journeys in the east. Further intelligence soon told him, however, that they were merely men, out to plunder. Moctezuma did not know whether to welcome or fight the new arrivals and he made the fatal error of allowing them into his capital city. The Spanish quickly took all he had in their search for gold and put him under house arrest. Soon after this he was killed, some accounts say by his own people, who thought he was collaborating with the invaders.

## Introduction
● Talk to the class about the conquest of the Aztec Empire. Explain how the Spanish soldiers entered Mexico and quickly overpowered the Aztecs, who were not expecting them to fight or kill them.
● Explain how, very soon after arriving in Mexico, the Spanish and Aztec leaders met.
● Talk about how we can begin to understand the experiences of the Aztecs by re-creating what happened.

## Main teaching activity
● Help the children to make simple props. Model 'pyramids' can be made using boxes; a cross could be made from gold card; feathers will be needed for the Aztec headdresses. Create dramatic music for the arrival of Moctezuma using a drum and other percussion instruments.
● Use the costumes and objects that the children have made for role play of key events, such as the meeting between Cortés and Moctezuma and the eventual defeat of the Aztecs.
● Children could write up their scenes, either individually or in pairs.

## Plenary
● Act out the children's scenes in an assembly or to another class.

## Differentiation
Provide additional adult support during the writing activities.

# Understanding Aztec poetry

**Objectives**
● To find out about the events, people and changes studied from poetry.

**Vocabulary**
tragic, lamenting, sorrow

**Resources**
The photocopiable sheet 'An Aztec poem: Flowers and Songs of Sorrow' on page 140.

**Links**
NLS Y3 Word level work: vocabulary extension by collecting new words from reading and work in other subjects.
NC English KS2: En1 (4a) to create, adapt and sustain different roles, individually and in groups.
NC PSHE & citizenship KS2: (4b) to think about the lives of people living in other places and times, and people with different values and customs.

## Background

The pieces of Aztec poetry that survive reveal much about the beliefs and feelings of the Aztecs. The poem 'Flowers and Songs of Sorrow' was written soon after the conquest of their empire. The Aztecs had seen their cities, temples, pyramids and much of their way of life, especially their religion, destroyed in a very short space of time. The poem reveals how dependent they were upon the idea that everything relied upon the will of the gods. They believed that their defeat must have happened because the gods were angry with them. The Aztecs believed that there were five worlds following on from each other. In their belief system, four had already been destroyed, and they were living in the final one. Only by continual sacrifice to the gods could they prevent the final, complete end of the world. This perhaps explains the savageness of their religious rites, in that they were prepared to do anything to satisfy the will of their gods.

## Introduction

● Introduce the class to the idea that the Aztecs had stories and poems, much as we do today.
● Explain that their poetry was quite different to ours, though, and often about their gods.
● Tell the class they are going to find out a little about what Aztec poetry was like.

## Main teaching activity

● Read to the children the poem 'Flowers and Songs of Sorrow' from the photocopiable sheet on page 140. You may need to read it more than once for the children to take it in.
● Ask the children to write down descriptive words and phrases to describe their own feelings after hearing the poem.
● Discuss with them the meaning of the poem, for example: it is about how the Aztecs felt after they had been conquered by the Spanish.
● Work together with the children to create a dramatic scene, mime or freeze frame about the Aztec defeat. Rehearse and use percussion instruments as part of the drama.
● Read the poem, or ask a child to read it, as a conclusion to the scene you have created.

## Plenary

● Act out the drama in an assembly or to another class.

## Differentiation

Support the less able writers with word cards and dictionaries during the writing activity. Encourage more able children to write about the poem more fully.

# Comparing accounts of the Aztecs

## Objectives
● To recognise that the past is represented and interpreted in different ways, and to give reasons for this.

## Vocabulary
interpret, interpretation, represent, version

## Resources
The photocopiable sheet 'Different accounts of the conquest of the Aztecs' on page 141, one per child and one copy enlarged; highlighters or coloured pens; blank cards.

## Background
These extracts from accounts written on opposing sides are perhaps a good way of introducing children to the important concept of interpretation in history. Children can begin to see that the historical account that is written often depends on the point of view of the author, rather than actual fact. This is one of the key skills of the National Curriculum for History, and also a fundamental skill in understanding the study of history in general.

## Introduction
● Talk to the class about the idea of interpretation. Explain how everyone who talks or writes about an event has their own point of view, and how this sometimes influences the way they write and what they write.
● Tell the class that in this lesson they are going to think about the following questions: *How are historical accounts different from each other? Why are they different?*

## Main teaching activity
● Divide the class into two groups. Provide each group with one half of the photocopiable sheet 'Different accounts of the conquest of the Aztecs' on page 141 - either 'The Fall of Tenochtitlan - an Aztec elegy' or the extract from a Spanish account written by Bernal Diaz.
● Working in their groups, ask the children to discuss, note and highlight in a different colour the key points in their account.
● Allow enough time for the children to complete the task and then ask each group to report back on their findings.
● Give out small cards to the children and ask them to write down the key words or phrases to describe the point of view of each writer.
● Discuss with the whole class the different views of the conquest that they have read and how historians' accounts can differ depending on the sources they use.

## Plenary
● Display enlarged versions of the two accounts, labelled with the children's 'key points' cards.

## Links
NLS Y3 T2 Text 17: to make clear notes.
NC English KS2: En2 (2a) to use inference and deduction; (2b) to look for meaning beyond the literal.

## Differentiation
Provide adult support for the less able writers and readers as required. Encourage more able children to write more detailed 'key points' cards.

# Pyramids and gods

## Objectives
● To find out about the events, people and changes studied from historic sites.

## Vocabulary
pyramid, site, temple

## Resources
Art materials for making pyramids; information books, videos or pictures of the pyramids at Teotihuacan and Tenochtitlan. Useful websites include www.mexperience.com/guide/archaeology/teotihuacan.htm, www.mexperience.com/inmexico/photos/3a/teo/02122932.JPG, www.new odysseyart.co.uk and www.mexicolore.co.uk

## Links
NC English KS2: En1 (3) to talk effectively as members of a group.
NC Art and design KS2: (1a) to record from experience and imagination, to select and record from first-hand observation and to explore ideas for different purposes.
NC ICT KS2: (1a) to talk about what information they need and how they can find and use it.

## Background
While the pyramids at Tenochtitlan were built in the 14th and 15th centuries by the Aztecs, the very large pyramids at Teotihuacan were built over a period of hundreds of years, thousands of years earlier. The Teotihuacan civilisation was one of the earliest known in the Valley of Mexico.

The building of pyramids for religious and burial purposes seems to have been a feature of all Meso-American civilisations. Those at Teotihuacan were built up in layers and recent archaeology suggests that there were chambers deep inside, which might have been created as burial chambers. The main purpose of the pyramids of the Sun and Moon, however, and of those in Tenochtitlan, was as a site for the sacrifice of many thousands of human victims, to provide blood for the gods.

## Introduction
● Ask the class: *Why did the Aztecs build large pyramids?* and ask them to think of as many different reasons as they can.

## Main teaching activity
● Show the class videos or pictures of the pyramids at Teotihuacan and Tenochtitlan.
● Discuss the scale of the buildings and how those at Teotihuacan might have been made, thousands of years ago.
● Look at the detail on the buildings, such as the carved serpents' heads and explain that these were images of some of the Aztec gods.
● Talk about what has been found inside the pyramids and what we know they were used for. Temples were built on the top of pyramids and humans were sacrificed on them - their dead bodies flung down the central staircase on each pyramid.
● Organise the class into groups to investigate Aztec pyramids in more detail, using information books, websites and pictures.
● The children could also research Aztec myths to further understand what kinds of motifs and decorations were used in their architecture.
● Provide a selection of art materials and encourage the children to work in their groups to design, plan and make their own models of Aztec pyramids.

## Plenary
● Display the children's models and discuss what the children have found out about Aztec gods and religion.

## Differentiation
Organise the class to work in mixed ability groups to provide support for the less able children. Encourage more able children to write a short paragraph to go alongside their model pyramid.

# What have we found out about the Aztecs?

## Objectives
- To recall, select and organise historical information.
- To use dates and historical vocabulary to describe the period studied.
- To communicate their knowledge and understanding of history in a variety of ways.

## Vocabulary
all the vocabulary from the topic

## Resources
The children's grids from Lesson 2; reference books as necessary.

## Links
NLS Y3 T2 Text 17: to make clear notes; Y4 T2 Text 23: to collect information from a variety of sources and present it one simple format.
NC English KS2: En1 (3) to talk effectively as members of a group.
NC PSHE & citizenship KS2: (4b) to think about the lives of people living in other places and times, and people with different values and customs.

## Background
At the beginning of the topic, the children completed the first two sections of a grid and pasted it into their books. This activity allows the children to look back at the topic and review what they have discovered. The lesson also provides an opportunity for you to assess the children's learning and to check their understanding of key historical skills and concepts.

## Introduction
- Explain to the class that in this lesson they are going to summarise on their grid what they have learned throughout the topic.
- They are going to have in mind the question: *What have we learned about the Aztecs?*

## Main teaching activity
- Ask the children to work in pairs or small groups and recall all that they can about the Aztecs now that they are at the end of the topic.
- As the children work, go round the groups, giving support in the discussions as necessary.
- Invite the children to then work individually to record what they have learned on their grids.
- Then ask the whole class to assist you in creating a mind map on the board of all of the apsects of the Aztec civilisation that they have learned about.
- Ask the children to return to their individual grids to see if they can add any further information and to fill in any gaps they may have had, using the mind map to help them.
- Walk around the class and monitor the children's progress. Encourage them to check if there is anything in the second column of their grid, 'What I want to know', that still needs to be investigated. If so, ask them where they think they might find out the information they require and encourage them to work towards filling in the final column of their grid.

## Plenary
- Ask individuals to share their findings with the rest of the class. Invite the children to say what they enjoyed learning most about the Aztecs, and what it was they found least interesting. Discuss the key differences between Aztec life and life today.

## Differentiation
Organise the class to work in mixed ability groups in order to provide peer support. Schedule extra writing time for the less able children so that they can complete their grids as fully as possible.

# How the Spanish explorers found the Aztecs

**COLUMBUS' ROUTE 1492**

**CORTÉS' ROUTE 1518-19**

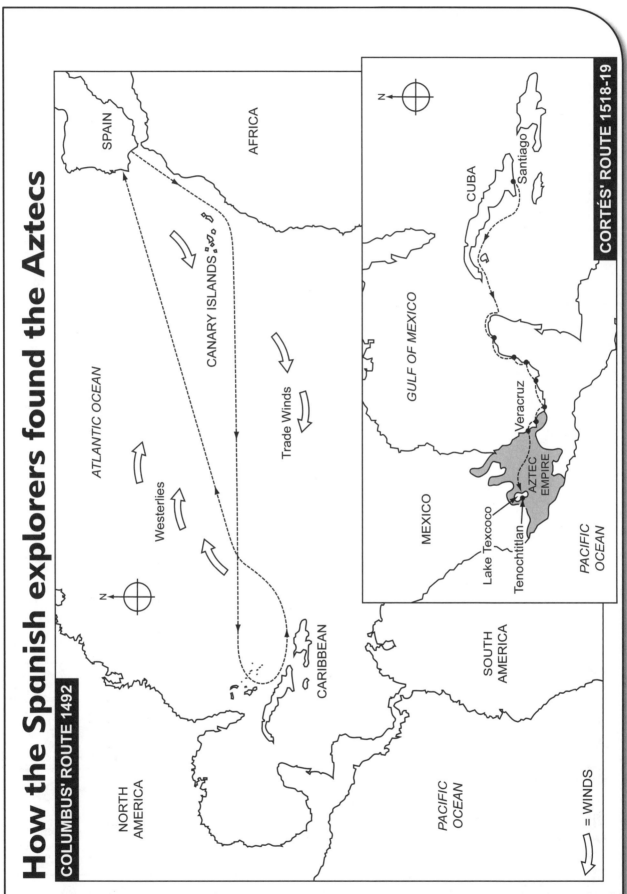

SPAIN

AFRICA

CANARY ISLANDS

Trade Winds

ATLANTIC OCEAN

Westerlies

N

NORTH AMERICA

CARIBBEAN

SOUTH AMERICA

PACIFIC OCEAN

CUBA

Santiago

GULF OF MEXICO

MEXICO

Veracruz

AZTEC EMPIRE

Lake Texcoco

Tenochtitlan

PACIFIC OCEAN

N

= WINDS

© The Drawing Room

# Aztec timeline

Cut out the boxes and complete this timeline of the Aztecs.

| 1492 | 1521 | 1519 | 1502 | 1525 | 1520 | 1325 | 1440 |
|------|------|------|------|------|------|------|------|
| Columbus sails to the Americas | The Aztecs are finally defeated by the Spanish | Cortés arrives on the coast of Mexico | Moctezuma II is crowned Emperor | Death of Cuauhtémoc, the last Aztec Emperor | Moctezuma II is killed and the Spanish leave Tenochtitlan | The Aztecs begin to create their capital city of Tenochtitlan | Moctezuma I begins his reign and the Aztec Empire is born |

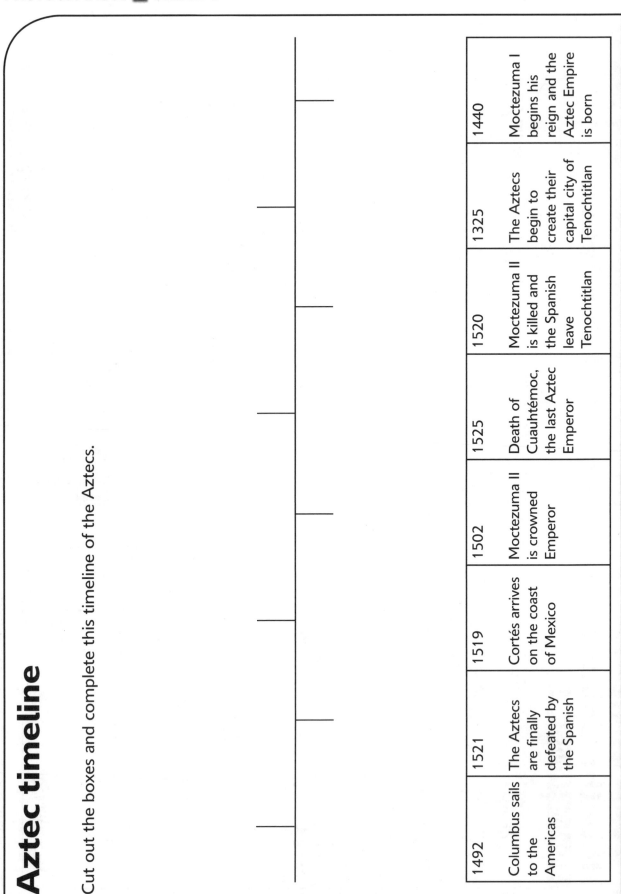

# An artist's idea of what Tenochtitlan looked like

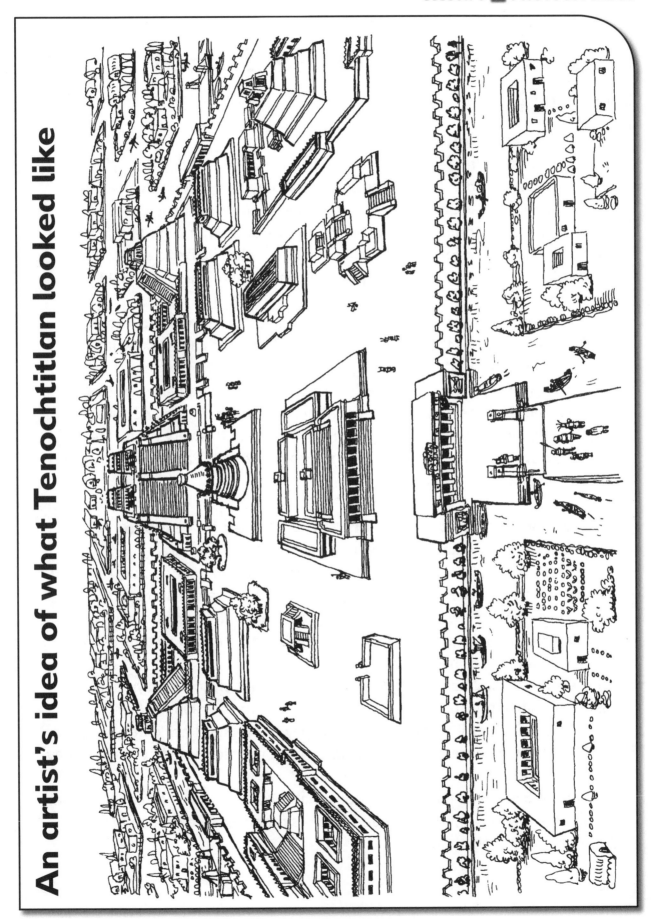

# How the Aztecs chose a place to settle

## The Aztec creation myth

In the distant past the Aztecs, or Mexica as they were called, left their home in the north and began to travel southwards. They had lived in the caves of Aztlan for many years, but their gods had told them they must leave.

They wandered for many years in the wild lands of the north, until one day, their god said: "Look for an eagle holding a serpent in its beak, seated on a cactus plant. When you see this sign, then this is where you must build your capital city."

They continued to wander in the very dry lands of Mexico and, eventually, they saw exactly what the god had described. There was an eagle, with a serpent in its mouth, sitting on a nopal cactus plant. Unfortunately, the cactus plant was growing right in the middle of a large lake called Lake Texcoco.

However, the beliefs of the Aztecs in their gods was very powerful and, undefeated, they went on to build their capital city in this very place. Their capital is now called Mexico City, after the name 'Mexica', and it is one of the largest cities in the world.

## Reasons why the Aztecs might have settled in Texcoco

The Aztecs, from the earliest times that we know of them, practised a very strict, fierce religion. Because they believed that the sun needed human blood to enable it to rise each morning, they carried out human sacrifices, sometimes killing many people in just one ceremony. This practice made them very unpopular amongst other tribes as they often sacrificed victims from other tribes that they had captured.

The Aztecs also had a habit of treating important visitors badly, as in the case of a visiting princess who was to be married to their king. When her father, the neighbouring ruler, heard that they had treated her cruelly and then killed her, he ordered that the entire Aztec people should be driven away from his kingdom.

It might have been for these reasons that the Aztecs were forced to move to live on a swampy, snake-infested island – simply because no one wanted them nearby, as neighbours.

# What the Aztecs looked like

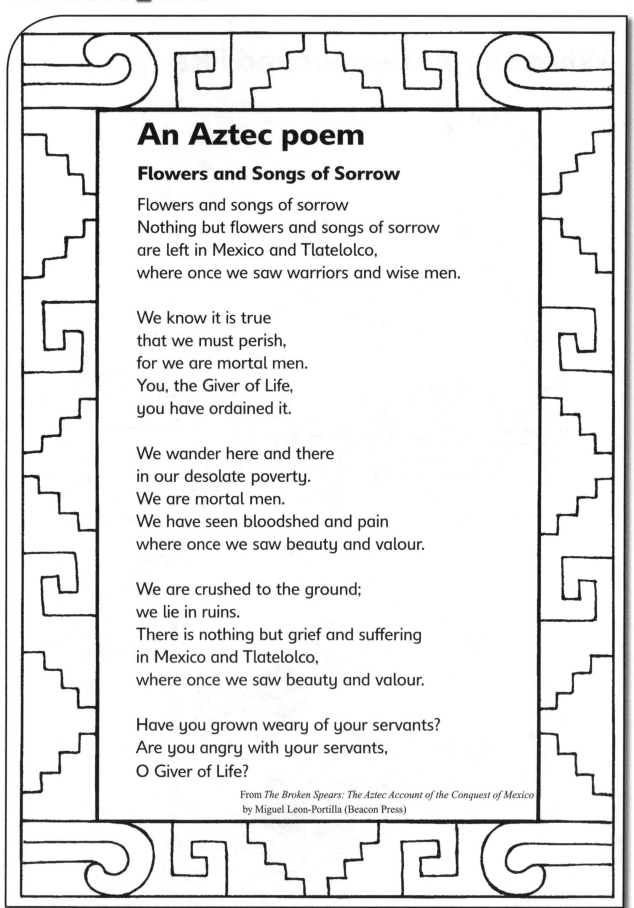

# An Aztec poem

## Flowers and Songs of Sorrow

Flowers and songs of sorrow
Nothing but flowers and songs of sorrow
are left in Mexico and Tlatelolco,
where once we saw warriors and wise men.

We know it is true
that we must perish,
for we are mortal men.
You, the Giver of Life,
you have ordained it.

We wander here and there
in our desolate poverty.
We are mortal men.
We have seen bloodshed and pain
where once we saw beauty and valour.

We are crushed to the ground;
we lie in ruins.
There is nothing but grief and suffering
in Mexico and Tlatelolco,
where once we saw beauty and valour.

Have you grown weary of your servants?
Are you angry with your servants,
O Giver of Life?

From *The Broken Spears: The Aztec Account of the Conquest of Mexico*
by Miguel Leon-Portilla (Beacon Press)

# Different accounts of the conquest of the Aztecs

### The Fall of Tenochtitlan – an Aztec elegy

Our cries of grief rise up
and our tears rain down,
for Tlatelolco is lost.
The Aztecs are fleeing across the lake;
they are running away like women.

How can we save our homes, my people?
The Aztecs are deserting the city:
the city is in flames, and all
is darkness and destruction.

Weep, my people:
know that with these disasters
we have lost the Mexican nation.
The water has turned bitter,
our food is bitter!
These are the acts of the Giver of Life...

From *The Broken Spears: The Aztec Account of the Conquest of Mexico* by Miguel Leon-Portilla (Beacon Press)

### An extract from a Spanish account

Now to speak of the dead bodies and heads that were in the houses where Guatemoc (sic) had taken refuge. I solemnly swear that all the houses and stockades in the lake were full of heads and corpses. I do not know how to describe it but it was the same in the streets and courts of Tlatelolco. We could not walk without treading on the bodies and heads of dead Indians. I have read about the destruction of Jerusalem, but I do not think the mortality was greater there than here in Mexico...

Indeed, the stench was so bad that no one could endure it, and for that reason each of us captains returned to his camp after Guatemoc's capture; even Cortés was ill from the odours which assailed his nostrils and from headache during those days in Tlatelolco.

The soldiers in the launches came off best and gained most spoil, because they were able to go to the houses in certain quarters of the lake where they knew there was cloth, gold and treasure. They also searched the reed beds in which the Mexicans had hidden their property. ...When Cortés demanded Moctezuma's treasure from Guatemoc and his captains, they told him that the men in the launches had stolen most of it.

From *The Conquest of New Spain* by Bernal Diaz (Penguin Books)

# CHAPTER 8

# Indus Valley

This chapter deals with an ancient civilisation, which stretched through the area now occupied by modern-day Pakistan and into parts of India and Afghanistan along the course of the River Indus. It dates from a period contemporary with that of the Ancient Egyptians.

Unknown to western society until the mid-19th century, the Indus Valley civilisation only began to be systematically excavated during the 1920s and 1930s and then by the archaeologist Sir Mortimer Wheeler in the 1950s. The chapter shows how archaeologists can create an account of a civilisation from the distant past using little evidence. It provides opportunities for children to use artefacts to understand the way of life of a lost civilisation and enables children to begin to understand how interpretations of historical evidence can and do differ.

| | OBJECTIVES | MAIN ACTIVITY |
|---|---|---|
| **Lesson 1** | To identify and describe reasons for events, situations and changes. To recall, select and organise historical information. | Children locate the Indus Valley area on the map, look at pictures and create a mind map of what they know. |
| **Lesson 2** [P] | To place events, people and changes into correct periods of time. To use dates and vocabulary relating to the passing of time. To communicate their knowledge in a variety of ways. | After working on a class timeline the children create their own, using history reference books. |
| **Lesson 3** [P] | To know about characteristic features of the period studied. To ask and answer questions, and to select and record information. To find out about the past from archaeology. | Children learn about two of the archaeologists and the excavation of Mohenjo-Daro. |
| **Lesson 4** | To recognise that the past is interpreted in different ways. To ask and answer questions, and to select and record information. | Children use questioning techniques to learn about the Indus Valley civilisation. |
| **Lesson 5** [P] | To find out about the past from maps, plans, photographs and other sources. | Using pictures of Mohenjo-Daro's streets, children make an illustration to scale and conduct research in groups. |
| **Lesson 6** [P] | To find out the past from plans, photographs and other sources. To communicate their knowledge in a variety of ways. | A site plan helps children to consider what it would be like to live in Mohenjo-Daro. |
| **Lesson 7** [P] | To find out about the past from artefacts. To ask and answer questions, and to select and record information. | Children look at an image of a chariot, consider what it was used for, and draw pictures or make models. |
| **Lesson 8** [P] | To find out about the past from artefacts. To ask and answer questions, and to select and record information. | Children research an image of weights and scales and write from a trader's point of view. |
| **Lesson 9** [P] | To recall, select and organise historical information. To communicate their knowledge in a variety of ways. | Children classify artefacts, create a display and write an archaeologist's report. |
| **Lesson 10** [P] | To find out about the past from written sources. To recognise that the past is interpreted in different ways. | Children study pictograms and seals and make a clay tablet containing a design of their own. |
| **Lesson 11** [P] | To find out about the past from artefacts. To communicate their knowledge in a variety of ways. | Using artefacts, children make inferences about life in the Indus Valley and produce 'tour guide' notes for a presentation. |
| **Lesson 12** | To recall, select and organise historical information. To communicate their knowledge in a variety of ways. | Children complete the mind maps they began in Lesson 1, filling in what they have now learned. |

# The Indus Valley and its features

## Objectives
● To identify and describe reasons, and results of, historical events, situations, and changes in the period studied.
● To recall, select and organise historical information.

## Vocabulary
river, valley, region, terrain

## Resources
Map or globe of the world; map of India and Pakistan; pictures showing the landscape, see http://www. peterlanger.com/countries/ Asia/Pakistan.index.htm; pens (different colours) and paper.

## Links
NC Geography KS2: (1a) to ask geographical questions; (2a) to use appropriate geographical vocabulary; (2c) to use atlases and globes, and maps and plans at a range of scales.

## Background
The River Indus is one of the great rivers of the Indian subcontinent. It runs from the Himalayas in Tibet to the Arabian Sea and is about 3000km long. Between about 2500BC and 1500BC the ancient Harrapan civilisation developed along its banks and those of its tributaries, using the water source and flood waters for farming. It was a similar development to that of the ancient Egyptian civilisation, which grew up along the Nile. This was an extensive civilisation that extended into India, Pakistan and Afghanistan. The two major cities that have been discovered to date are Mohenjo-Daro and Harrapa.

## Introduction
● Explain to the class that this topic is about a place called the Indus Valley, through which the River Indus runs.
● Ask if anyone has been there or knows where it is. (Some children of Pakistani origin may be familiar with the region.)
● Ask if anyone knows what it is like in this part of the world. Prompt the children with questions such as: *What is this region like today? What do we already know about it?*

## Main teaching activity
● Locate the Indus Valley on a map and explain that this is now in modern-day Pakistan. Discuss how far it is from Britain and look at the other countries that are nearby, such as India and Afghanistan.
● Next, look at a larger scale map of the area, showing India and Pakistan. Look at the terrain and note the mountainous areas, deserts, rivers and oceans.
● Look at pictures and photographs of the landscape and talk about how this could have affected settlement and lifestyles. Discuss why people would have settled there. (Refer to the children's knowledge of Ancient Egypt if they have already done this as a topic.)
● Talk about how the River Indus was, and still is, very useful for its water supply, but also discuss its problems, such as the frequent flooding that takes place and the consequences of this.
● Begin to draw a mind map of what is already known about the topic.

## Plenary
● Allow time for the children to draw their own mind maps. Discuss other things that are not yet on the mind map and leave spaces for these to be added. Encourage the children to classify the information.

## Differentiation
Provide additional adult support for children with special needs during the writing activity.

# When was the Indus Valley civilisation?

## Objectives
- To place events, people and changes into correct periods of time.
- To use dates and vocabulary relating to the passing of time.
- To communicate their knowledge and understanding of history in a variety of ways.

## Vocabulary
ancient, modern, civilisation, BC, ad

## Resources
The photocopiable sheet 'Indus Valley timeline' on page 155, one per child and one enlarged for class work; scissors; glue; A3 paper; information books such as *The Indus Valley Civilisation* by Rhona Dick (Evans Brothers).

## Links
NNS Y3-4: number sequences, place value and ordering.
NLS Y5 T2 Text 16: to prepare for reading by identifying what they already know and what they need to find out; T2 Text 17: to locate information confidently and efficiently.

## Background
The Indus Valley civilisation is considered to be ancient because it pre-dates the birth of Christ by many centuries and is contemporary with part of the ancient Egyptian period. Time is a difficult concept for young children to comprehend and, for this reason, timeline activities are used to try to help them make sense of the great time spans involved in this topic. By this stage in children's learning some will be beginning to understand the significance of dates but they are still likely to need considerable support in using them on a timeline and in ordering events chronologically, particularly over the bc/AD divide. The assembling of information on the class timeline is suggested as a whole-class activity so you can support the children in this skill.

## Introduction
- Talk about how the Indus Valley civilisation is called 'ancient'. Discuss the meaning of the word 'ancient' (for example, from a time long ago in the past).
- Ask if anyone can estimate, in centuries or thousands of years, an answer to the question: *When was the Indus Valley civilisation?*

## Main teaching activity
- Look at a large class version of the photocopiable sheet 'Indus Valley timeline' on page 155 and revise the use of bc and AD.
- Discuss the period of the Indus Valley civilisation and point out the span of time it covered.
- Add to the timeline details from other topics in history that the children have covered to help them locate the period of time in relation to their existing knowledge. These could include information about Ancient Egypt, the Romans, The Tudors, or any other topic.
- Give each child a copy of the photocopiable sheet, scissors and glue and ask them to begin to construct their own longer timelines, perhaps covering three sheets of A3 paper. Provide a variety of information books for the children to use as reference material about historical periods they have studied in the past.

## Plenary
- Talk about any other information they have added to their timelines. Emphasise different time spans, for example: Tudor voyages of discovery took place about 4000 years after the start of the Indus Valley civilisation began.

## Differentiation
The less able will require support in creating timelines. Challenge the more able to find specific information to add to their timelines.

# The first archaeologists at the Indus Valley

## Objectives
● To know about characteristic features of the period studied.
● To ask and answer questions, and to select and record information relevant to the focus of the enquiry.
● How to find out about the events, people and changes studied from archaeology.

## Vocabulary
archaeology, archaeologist, excavation

## Resources
The photocopiable sheet 'Archaeologists in the Indus Valley' on page 156, one per child; pictures of archeologists working on excavations (see www. harappa.com/indus2/index. html); photographs of modern-day buildings (see http://geo.ya.com/travel images/pakistan.html); pictures of houses and streets that are thought to have existed in the Indus Valley from books such as *The Indus Valley (Excavating the Past)* by Ilona Aronovsky and Sujata Gopinath (Heinemann) and *History 7* in the *Ready Resources* series (Scholastic).

## Links
NLS Y5 T2 Text 17: to locate information confidently and efficiently. NC English KS2: En1 (3) to talk effectively as members of a group.

## Background
Sir Mortimer Wheeler was known for the systematic methods he used for dating objects according to the levels and locations of their discovery. This has become an accepted method for enquiry, recording and dating archaeological finds. Sir Mortimer Wheeler also published books about his work and made the study of archaeology very popular through his television broadcasts about it. He worked on Roman archaeological sites in Britain as well as being the first, in the 1950s, following the earlier excavations of Ernest Mackay, to organise systematic enquiry into the sites of the Indus Valley civilisation at Mohenjo-Daro and Harappa.

## Introduction
● Tell the class that in this lesson they are gong to learn about the work of people called archaeologists.
● Discuss the meaning of the word and talk about what kind of work archaeologists do.

## Main teaching activity
● Discuss the archaeologists who worked on Mohenjo-Daro: Mr Ernest Mackay and Sir Mortimer Wheeler.
● Show the class pictures of the sites and illustrations of the people working there. Ask the children if they think it would be easy or difficult to learn about the people who lived in the Indus Valley from excavating sites, such as those shown in the pictures.
● Provide pictures of the houses and streets that are thought to have existed, alongside pictures of similar modern-day buildings. Ask the children to make comparisons – what are the similarities and differences?
● Give the children copies of the photocopiable sheet 'Archaeologists in the Indus Valley' on page 156.
● Ask the children to read the passage about Sir Mortimer Wheeler and answer the questions about it.

## Plenary
● Ask the children how they think the archaeologists worked out their conclusions. Discuss the possibility that other archaeologists might disagree. Talk about the notion of interpretation and how this can differ in studying the past.

## Differentiation
Match the questioning to suit the differing abilities within the class. Provide further support for the less able children with interpreting the visual resources and reading the photocopiable sheet as needed.

# Using archaeology to find out about Mohenjo-Daro

## Objectives
● To recognise that the past is represented and interpreted in different ways, and to give reasons for this.
● To ask and answer questions, and to select and record information relevant to the focus of the enquiry.

## Vocabulary
interpret, interpretation, evidence

## Resources
Plans, maps and pictures of the findings at Mohenjo-Daro, using books, for example *The Indus Valley (Excavating the Past)* by Ilona Aronovsky and Sujata Gopinath (Heinemann) and websites such as www.bbc.co.uk/schools/indusvalley/flash/ivl3_index.shtml

## Links
NLS Y5 T1 Text 26: to make notes for different purposes; T1 Text 27: to use simple abbreviations in note-taking.
NC English KS2: En1 (3) to talk effectively as members of a group.

## Background
Archaeologists have to work strictly with the evidence that they find in the ground. They follow a process of inductive reasoning, using other information and knowledge, along with detailed questioning, to work out the significance of objects. For example, questions about the type of material that an object is made of will help the archaeologist to work out the function and place of the object. They can also make assumptions through inferences about society based on the objects found. For example, the discovery of some very elaborate jewellery suggests that some people were rich and that they were particular about their appearance. This lesson asks children to begin to use the techniques of archaeology to question objects found at Mohenjo-Daro.

## Introduction
● Ask the class what sort of things they would want to know if they discovered a lost city. Explain that these are the sorts of questions Sir Mortimer Wheeler and his colleagues asked themselves.

## Main teaching activity
● List the questions the children thought of, then discuss whether archaeology would be able to provide answers to all of them.
● Play the 'Skeleton game'. Ask a child to lie in the middle of the floor and ask the others to think what would be left of the child and their belongings after 3000 years. They will need to realise that some things survive such as bone and pottery, but not fabrics, paper and so on.
● Look again at the list of questions and decide which ones an archaeologist might ask. For example: *What objects will still be there after 3000 years? What sort of materials will survive for that long?*
● Give out to each child a three-column chart and in the first column, ask them to write the heading 'Questions an archaeologist could ask'. Then invite the children to write in the column some archaeologist's questions about Mohenjho-Daro derived from the class discussions.
● Ask them to write the heading 'Things an archaeologist might find' in the second column. The children can work in pairs to list objects an archaeologist might find in a city that has been buried for 3000 years.

## Plenary
● Explain that the third column of their chart needs to be headed 'Things that were found at Mohenjo-Daro'. They can complete this column as they work on the topic. (Remember to refer back to the charts over the course of the lessons and encourage its completion.)

## Differentiation
Working in mixed ability pairs will provide support for the less able.

# Plans of the city

## Objectives
● To find out about the events, people and changes studied from photographs and a range of other sources of information.

## Vocabulary
excavate, aerial photograph

## Resources
The photocopiable sheet 'A street in Mohenjo-Daro' on page 157, enlarged for class work; sheets of paper or long pieces of cloth; photographs of the streets of Mohenjo-Daro from books, resource packs and websites such as http://www.ancientindia.co.uk/indus/explore/his03.html and www.bbc.co.uk/schools/indusvalley/html/ivl3_find.shtml

## Links
NLS Y6 T1 Text 17: to write non-chronological reports linked to other subjects.
NC English KS2: En1 (3) to talk effectively as members of a group.
NC PSHE & citizenship KS2: (4b) to think about the lives of people living in other places and times, and people with different values and customs.

## Background
The city of Mohenjo-Daro was built about 5000 years ago and was inhabited for about 600 or 700 years. There seems to have been a high and low town, with a citadel in the highest part. In the lower town there are wide streets and narrow lanes and a mixture of large and small houses. High walls still remain, carefully built from bricks, and the wide main streets can be clearly seen on the plan of the city. Sir Mortimer Wheeler believed that they might have joined up to form a grid. It is possible that the city had been carefully designed and laid out like modern towns.

## Introduction
● Talk about the streets where the children live and think about what streets are like in many places in Britain (for example: winding and bending; all different shapes and sizes and so on).
● Tell the class that the streets that have been excavated in Mohenjo-Daro were quite different from these and that in this lesson they are going to find out what they were like.

## Main teaching activity
● Study carefully with the class examples of the photographs taken following the excavations at Mohenjo-Daro.
● Discuss the shape and size of the buildings and streets, as these can be worked out from the photographs.
● Look at the photocopiable sheet 'A street in Mohenjo-Daro' on page 157. Discuss what can be found out from this picture.
● Find a large space in the school and make an illustration to scale of part of one Mohenjo-Daro street, using sheets of paper or long pieces of cloth to mark out the walls.
● Look at the width of the street and discuss why it was designed like this.
● Talk about the way streets would have been planned to suit the climate and conditions in the area.
● Organise the children to work in pairs or small groups to research further into what the streets and buildings were like.
● Ask the children to keep a record of their research, the sources they have used and the information they have found out.

## Plenary
● Look at other photographs of the streets as they are now. Ask volunteers to suggest what kinds of traffic would have used these streets. Consider what reasons there might have been for making the main streets wide and straight.

## Differentiation
Working in mixed ability pairs will provide support for the less able.

# Life in Mohenjo-Daro

## Objectives
● To find out about the events, people and changes studied from plans, photographs and a range of other sources of information.
● To communicate their knowledge and understanding of history in a variety of ways.

## Vocabulary
sewer, hygiene, sanitation

## Resources
The photocopiable sheet 'Site plan of Mohenjo-Daro' on page 158, enlarged for class work; reference material about life in Mohenjo-Daro, using websites such as www.ancientindia.co.uk/indus/explore/images/cit0.gif or www.asiasociety.org/arts/exhibitions_indus_valley.html

## Links
NLS Y6 T1 Text 15: to develop a journalistic style.
NC English KS2: En1 (3) to talk effectively as members of a group.
NC PSHE & citizenship KS2: (4b) to think about the lives of people living in other places and times, and people with different values and customs.

## Background
Many aspects of life in Mohenjo-Daro seem, from looking at the site plan, very similar to life in cities throughout history. There appears to have been a more crowded, poorer area and a higher section, containing larger, more important buildings. Society seems to have included both rich and poor. What is remarkable about Mohenjo-Daro is the elaborate system of drains bringing clean water into even the smaller houses and the sewers that took away dirty water. Homes also seem to have had a room for bathing and many had their own private well. All this suggests that, for the relatively short time the city was occupied, its inhabitants led fairly healthy, comfortable lives.

## Introduction
Ask the children: *What was it like to live in a city like Mohenjo-Daro?*

## Main teaching activity
● Look at an enlarged copy of the photocopiable sheet 'Site plan of Mohenjo-Daro' on page 158. Use this to locate large buildings, such as the granary, citadel and great bath.
● Discuss why the city was laid out with the streets in a grid pattern. Perhaps it had been carefully planned; maybe this was what towns were like in that part of the world. (Point out that empty spaces on the plan idicate areas that have not yet been excavated.)
● Can the children think of any towns or cities today built on a grid pattern? (For example: Milton Keynes and New York.)
● In ancient times the city was not as near to the River Indus as it is now, because the river has changed its course. Ask why the children think it was built some distance away from the water (to avoid flooding).
● Discuss the facilties that the houses in Mohenjo-Daro had, such as drains, sewers and kilns.
● Ask the children why the houses are designed with very little window area, especially on the street-side of the houses. (For example: for privacy; perhaps to keep the houses quiet and cool.)
● Talk about the climate in Mohenjo-Daro during the summer months.
● Organise the class to work in pairs and to carry out further research into what it would have been like to live in a city like this.
● Ask the children to record their findings in the form of a newspaper article.

## Plenary
● Ask for volunteers to describe what it would have been like to live in Mohenjo-Daro, especially in the great heat of summer.

## Differentiation
Working in mixed ability pairs will provide support for the less able.

# What can we learn from objects?

## Objectives
● To find out about the events, people and changes studied from artefacts.
● To ask and answer questions, and to select and record information relevant to the focus of the enquiry.

## Vocabulary
chariot, bronze, pottery

## Resources
Paper and art materials; enlarged picture of the chariot on the photocopiable sheet 'Indus Valley artefacts' on page 159; other pictures of artefacts from the Indus Valley, using websites such as www.ancientindia.co.uk/indus and www.harappa.com/har/har0.html

## Links
NC Art and design KS2: (1a) to record from experience and imagination, to select and record from first-hand observation and to explore ideas for different purposes; (2c) to use a variety of methods to design and make images and artefacts.
NC English KS2: En1 (3) to talk effectively as members of a group.

## Background
Many artefacts made of pottery and metal have survived over the thousands of years since the Indus Valley civilisation flourished. Several terracotta animals on wheels and toy carts have been found at Mohenjo-Daro and other sites, as well as a model chariot. This chariot was probably made of bronze and was in good condition when it was found. It shows how oxen were used to pull carts and vehicles. The use of the wheel was clearly well understood and it seems that people were beginning to develop technology to meet their needs. In this lesson the children will consider the chariot as an artefact and use it to ask and answer questions about transport and technology.

## Introduction
● Explain that in this lesson the children are going to learn about transport in the Indus Valley.
● They are going to explore the question: *What were chariots like in the Indus Valley civilisation?*

## Main teaching activity
● Look at the photocopiable sheet 'Indus Valley artefacts' on page 159. Explain that some terracotta toys have been found at Mohenjo-Daro and also a small bronze chariot.
● Discuss what it was used for and who would have used it. Point out that no one really knows for certain and that there could be several different answers.
● Can the children think what such a chariot might have been made from?
● Does it remind them of chariots they have seen from other parts of the world?
● Give the children art paper to draw pictures of their ideas about how the chariot might have been used. Alternatively, provide art and craft materials or clay for children to make 3D models of a chariot.

## Plenary
● Ask the children to show their pictures and share their ideas about how the chariot might have been used. Consider the idea that it might not have been a chariot at all but a vehicle used with a plough for farming the muddy land. The ploughman might not have wanted to work with wet feet all day!

## Differentiation
Allow time for the children to talk about their designs in order to provide additional support for the less able. More able children might write explanations of how their chariots were used.

# Indus Valley weights

## Objectives
● To find out about the events, people and changes studied from artefacts.
● To ask and answer questions, and to select and record information relevant to the focus of the enquiry.

## Vocabulary
weights, chert, measurement

## Resources
Enlarged picture of weights and hand scales on the photocopiable sheet 'Indus Valley artefacts' on page 159; modern scales.

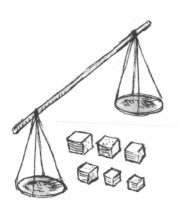

## Links
NLS Y5 T3 Text 19: to construct an argument to persuade others of a point of view.
NC ICT KS2: (3a) to share and exchange information in a variety of forms.

## Background
Many sets of weights like the ones illustrated on the photocopiable sheet on page 159 have been found in Indus Valley cities. They were made from stone such as chert and were probably used for measuring the weight of grain and other foodstuffs on balancing scales. The scales were often made of two copper plates suspended from a wooden stick. The weights would go on one plate and whatever was being weighed would go on the other. The manufacture of these weights suggests an advanced society where craft skills were quite sophisticated. It also suggests that there was a strong belief in fairness, since so many of these weights have been discovered, indicating that it was likely to have been standard practice to carefully weigh goods, possibly for sale.

## Introduction
● Tell the class that numerous weights have been found in the course of the excavations in the Indus Valley. Some are in complete sets, increasing in size.
● Explain that this lesson will focus on the question: *What can we learn from weights that have been found?*

## Main teaching activity
● Look at the enlarged picture of the weights on the photocopiable 'Indus Valley artefacts' on page 159.
● Ask for suggestions as to what they might be and explain that they are carefully cut stones, which were used as weights.
● Tell the class that these have been found throughout the region.
● Ask the children how they think the stones might have been used with simple scales.
● Show the picture of the scales (also on the photocopiable sheet) and discuss how the weights would have been used on this. Compare them with sets of scales in school.
● Discuss what might have been weighed using them.
● Prompt the children to think why these weights were used so widely. What does this tell us about the people and their way of life?
● Challenge the children to write an argument from the point of view of a trader where the weight-maker has made his weights too heavy.

## Plenary
● Share one or two of the children's arguments with the class. Compiling a web page containing their points of view is a good opportunity to incorporate ICT.

## Differentiation
Provide additional adult support for children with special needs during the writing and ICT activity.

# Classifying artefacts

## Objectives
● To recall, select and organise historical information.
● To communicate their knowledge and understanding of history in a variety of ways.

## Vocabulary
sort, organise, classify, evidence

## Resources
Large sheets of paper; pens; glue or Blu-Tack; the photocopiable sheet 'Indus Valley artefacts' on page 159, one per child and one copy enlarged for class work; selection of pictures and photographs from books and websites such as www.harappa.com/har/har0.html, www.bbc.co.uk/schools/indusvalley/flash/ivl3_index.shtml and www.ancientindia.co.uk/indus/explore/l_intro.html

## Links
NLS Y6 T1 Text 17: to write non-chronological reports linked to other subjects.
NC English KS2: En1 (3) to talk effectively as members of a group.

## Background
The classification of artefacts is important for many reasons. Firstly, classification according to the spot where they are found is important, since this can be crucial to the dating process. Classification according to the properties of the artefacts can also be useful in finding out what sort of manufacturing or technology was used. Another classification would be according to the function of the objects, since this can tell us a great deal about the daily lives of the people that used them.

## Introduction
● Talk about the wide range of items that have been found during the excavations in the Indus Valley. Ask the children to recall as many as they can.
● Explain that these objects could be sorted and organised in many different ways, in order, for example, to make a museum display.
● Tell the class that in this lesson they are going to think about how they would make a museum display. This means that they will need to think about how many different ways they can classify the artefacts they have seen.

## Main teaching activity
● Show the class enlarged images of artefacts from the Indus Valley, including those on the photocopiable sheet on page 159.
● Discuss how the artefacts might be sorted into groups, for example: according to the materials they are made from; what they might have been used for, and so on.
● Organise the class to work in small groups and allocate a theme to each group, such as: fashion, leisure, work, transport, important people, writing and animals.
● Ask the children to select and cut out pictures that relate to their theme, from the photocopiable sheet and from any other sources that they have.
● Provide the children with a large sheet of paper on a display board on which to organise their objects.
● Invite the children to then write an archaeologist's report, explaining why they have grouped the artefacts in this way and what they think their selection shows about the way of life of the Indus Valley people, adding this to their display.

## Plenary
● Ask the children to set out their displays and then rotate around the room, looking at the work of the other groups.

## Differentiation
Working in mixed ability pairs will provide support for the less able.

# Interpretations of picture writing

## Objectives
● To find out about the events, people and changes studied from written sources.
● To recognise that the past is represented and interpreted in different ways, and to give reasons for this.

## Vocabulary
seals, pictograms, ideograms

## Resources
Picture of the seal on the photocopiable sheet 'Indus Valley artefacts' on page 159, one per child and one enlarged for class work; range of pictures showing pictograms and seals from websites such as www. harappa.com/har/har0. html; art materials and clay.

## Links
NC Art and design KS2: (1a) to record from experience and imagination, to select and record from first-hand observation and to explore ideas for different purposes.

## Background
Stone seals containing pictures and signs have been found throughout the Indus Valley cities. The seal would have been pressed into clay to make an impression. Images of bulls, elephants, rhinos, a one-horned animal and compositions of various animals appear on the seals, which as yet remain largely undeciphered. It is thought that the one-horned animal may have been the sign of traders and that there may have been legends about it. Many pieces of clay stamped with seals have been found in buildings where goods were packed or kept, suggesting that they may have been the mark of the trader who supplied the goods, used to identify their ownership.

## Introduction
● Look at the enlarged picture of the seal on the photocopiable sheet 'Indus Valley artefacts' on page 159 and explain its use.
● Discuss the way the people of the Indus Valley had begun to develop a writing system using pictograms.
● Talk about what pictograms were and how they were carved into stone seals to pass on information.

## Main teaching activity
● Look at a selection of pictures of seals, including the one on the photocopiable sheet 'Indus Valley artefacts' on page 159.
● Discuss how it is possible to have different ideas and to create different interpretations of the pictograms, since no one fully knows what they mean.
● Tell the children that some people believe that the different images may have been the mark of a trader who supplied goods.
● Provide art materials and clay and ask the children to design their own pictogram and make a clay tablet containing their design.
● Ask the children to think carefully about their design first – perhaps sketching a few images first – before making their final model. The design should carry a 'clue' as to its meaning.

## Plenary
● Invite the children to pass their seal to a partner and see if they can work out its meaning.
● Make a display of the clay designs along with the pictures you looked at at the beginning of the lesson.

## Differentiation
Provide additional adult support for children with special needs as required. The children who complete their work more quickly can devise a range of pictograms.

# Learning from artefacts

## Objectives
- To find out about the events, people and changes studied from artefacts.
- To communicate their knowledge and understanding of history in a variety of ways.

## Vocabulary
guide, tour

## Resources
The photocopiable sheet 'Indus Valley artefacts' on page 159, one per child; pictures of artefacts from websites or books; computers with PowerPoint (optional).

## Links
NLS Y5 T1 Text 26: to make notes for different purposes.
NC ICT KS2: (3a) to share and exchange information in a variety of forms.

## Background
The activities in this lesson enable children to use their own inferential skills to work with pictures of artefacts and find out from them as much as they can about life in the Indus Valley. Having to make notes, summarise their thinking and then share them with the class encourages them to think carefully about the key points that they want to make and how to communicate these effectively.

## Introduction
- Explain to the class that in this lesson they are going to take on the role of a museum guide.
- They will need to make notes on the question: *What do the artefacts that have been found tell us about the people of the Indus Valley?*

## Main teaching activity
- Look at the images on the photocopiable sheet 'Artefacts from the Indus Valley' on page 159 and also some taken from websites and books.
- Working with the whole class, ask the children to make inferences about what life was like, using two or three artefacts as starting points. Explain how some things are not obvious, such as what the weights were, but that, after thinking and talking about them, sometimes their uses become clear.
- Discuss the sorts of questions that we can ask about artefacts. For example, questions might include:
    What does the pottery tell us about the lives people led?
    What does the model of the chariot show?
    What can we say about everyday life from looking at the weights and scales?
    Why were seals used and what does this tell us about the people who used them?
- Provide each child with a selection of artefacts and ask them to make notes on them about their uses, who might have used them and why. The purpose of the notes is to summarise everything they could say about their objects. They could scan in their pictures and make notes using PowerPoint.

## Plenary
- Ask a number of children to give their 'tour-guide talk' to the rest of the class. These talks could be spread throughout a week to provide a conclusion to lessons on artefacts from the Indus Valley.

## Differentiation
Provide additional adult support for children with special needs during the writing activity.

# What have we found out about the Indus Valley civilisation?

## Objectives
● To recall, select and organise historical information
● To communicate their knowledge and understanding of history in a variety of ways.

## Vocabulary
all the vocabulary from the topic

## Resources
The partly completed mind map from Lesson 1; selection of the work that has been carried out; resource packs, books and website resources.

## Background
Recalling and summarising what has been learned in the course of a theme or topic is an important part of the whole learning process. It enables the children to develop their memory skills and also their ability to draw out the key points from everything they have covered. If there is time, they will enjoy searching for further information to fill any gaps in their knowledge. The use of a mind map will encourage the children to focus on key words and phrases, which in turn will enable them to carry out further focused internet searches. They will also begin to sort and classify the information they have found.

## Introduction
● Explain that in this lesson the class is going to complete the mind map that they began at the start of the topic.
● Tell the children that they are going to work on the questions: *What have we found out about the Indus Valley civilisation? Have we found out anything of our own?*

## Main teaching activity
● Ask each child in turn what they have learned about the Indus Valley civilisation, either from lessons or from their own research on the internet and using books.
● This can become a game by requiring each child to contribute something different.
● Ask the children to then work in pairs to complete their mind maps. They will need to group and classify the information they add, for example, under different subjects.
● Observation of these activities provides useful assessment opportunities. Listen to conversations to assess children's conceptual understanding, their use of appropriate vocabulary and dates and their knowledge of the subject. The use of the mind map will enable you to assess children's abilities in summarising and communicating their learning concisely.

## Plenary
● Make a display of the completed mind maps and allow time for the children to look at each others' work.

## Differentiation
Provide additional adult support as required, for instance helping children to organise their ideas, spell words for their mind maps and so on.

## Links
NLS Y5 T1 Text 26: to make notes for different purposes.
NC PSHE & citizenship KS2: (4b) to think about the lives of people living in other places and times, and people with different values and customs.

# Indus Valley timeline

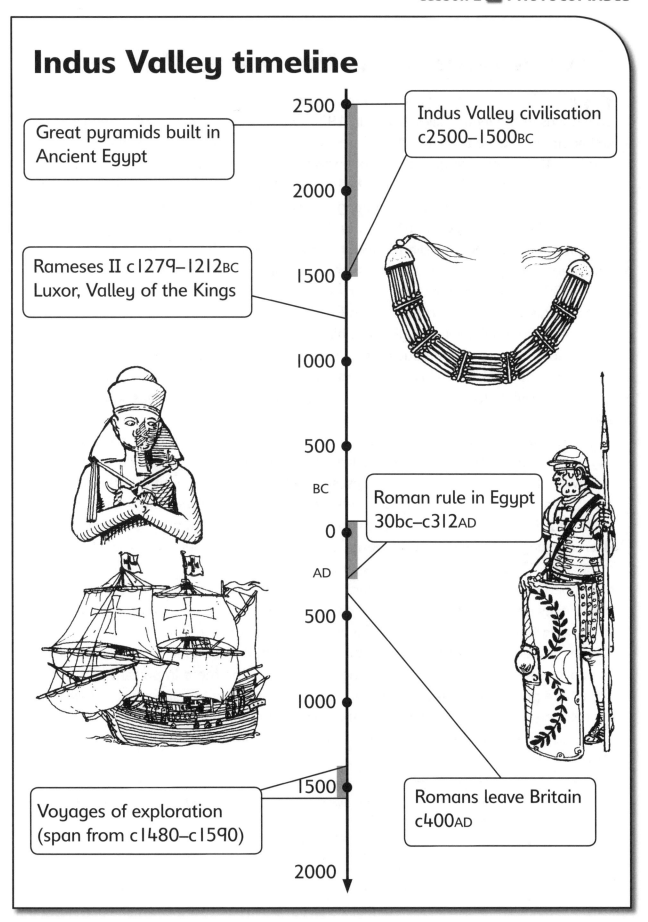

2500 — Indus Valley civilisation
c2500–1500BC

Great pyramids built in
Ancient Egypt

2000

1500

Rameses II c1279–1212BC
Luxor, Valley of the Kings

1000

500

BC

0 — Roman rule in Egypt
30bc–c312AD

AD

500

1000

1500 — Romans leave Britain
c400AD

Voyages of exploration
(span from c1480–c1590)

2000

# Archaeologists in the Indus Valley

During the 19th century people were aware that there were the remains of ancient towns in the Indus Valley. It was in 1920 when Rakhal Das Banerji, an Indian archaeologist, began to realise that there might be some remains of buildings underneath the many large mounds of earth found in the area. Between 1921 and 1922, Banerji began his excavations at Mohenjo-Daro. He soon discovered the remains of buildings and many artefacts, including beads, weights, pottery and seals.

Throughout the 1920s and 1930s, under the direction of Ernest Mackay, excavations continued, revealing a city of buildings built with bricks. In 1935 the excavations stopped because Mackay wanted to write up his report and it was not until 1950 that further work was undertaken by Sir Mortimer Wheeler, an archaeologist with a good reputation in Britain.

Sir Mortimer Wheeler brought with him new ideas about excavation and archaeology. He used systematic methods for marking finds and for dating them. He also used a method known as the 'box grid method', whereby squares of ground were excavated leaving full cross-sections intact between the excavated areas so that the earth layers could still be seen.

He found a number of streets in an area he called Lower Town that seemed to be laid out in a grid pattern, with some wide avenues leading through the centre and narrower alleys where most of the houses were located. He thought that this was the area where most of the ordinary people lived and worked because the houses were small and close together. There were many houses with their own private wells for clean drinking water and bathing rooms, with drains that led out into larger drains in the streets. These findings led Sir Mortimer to conclude that this had been a well-developed civilisation where people had high standards. The houses had several rooms that mostly opened out onto a central courtyard rather than onto the street, suggesting that the inhabitants liked to be private in their own homes.

On a mound almost twelve metres high, Sir Mortimer found large buildings, such as public baths and a granary, suggesting that this was the more important part of the city where public meetings and business took place along with religious activities. Wheeler named this the Citadel, but other archaeologists did not agree with some of the things he said. They thought he had misinterpreted the use of some of the buildings.

1. Why did people think that there must be something buried in the area before excavations began?
2. What sort of objects were the first to be excavated at Mohenjo-Daro?
3. What larger things were discovered by Mackay?
4. Why did Sir Mortimer Wheeler have a good reputation as an archaeologist?
5. What sort of civilisation did Sir Mortimer Wheeler think he had found?

# A street in Mohenjo-Daro

# Site plan of Mohenjo-Daro

Great Bath

Granary

Citadel
(on a mound)

Lower town

◣ SCHOLASTIC

# Indus Valley artefacts

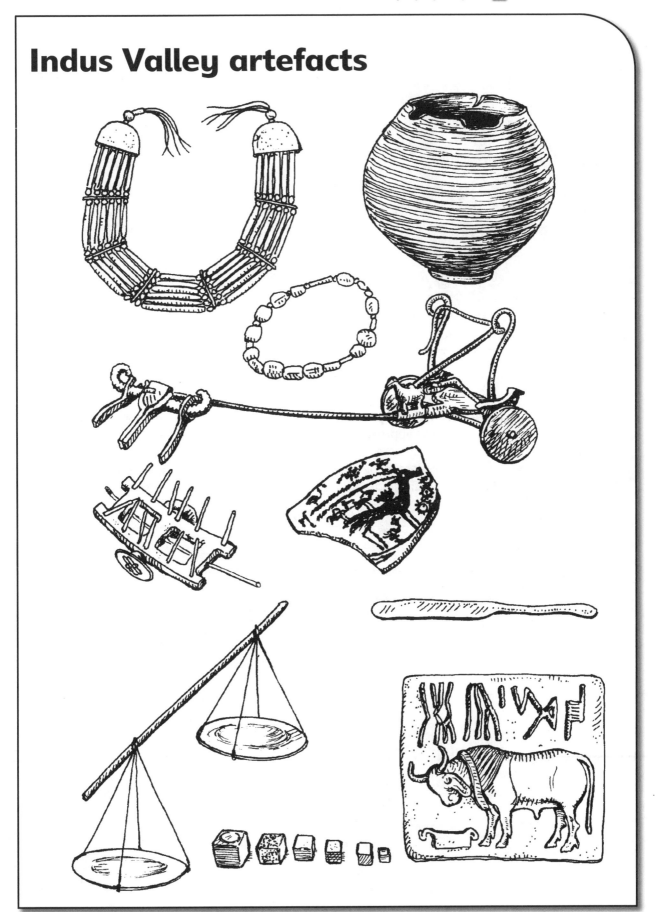

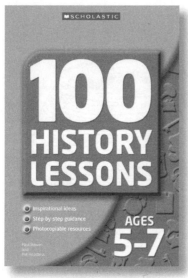
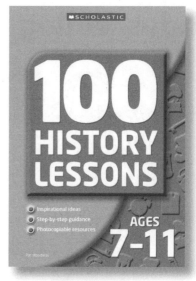